# Customer Engagement Officer (CEO): Content Marketing and the Realities of Executive Blogging

# Mark Hillary

Customer Engagement Officer (CEO):
Content Marketing and the Realities of Executive
Blogging

Published by Carnaby Books, São Paulo

Carnaby Books
IT Decisions Comunicação Editorial Ltda EPP
Avenida Professor Alfonso Bovero, 1443
São Paulo – SP
CEP 05019-010
Brazil

www.markhillary.com
facebook.com/markhillary
@markhillary

Quoc-Huy Nguyen Dinh photographed the author portrait featured in this book: www.qhphotography.com.

The cover was conceived and designed by Sean Cook at Level 3 Creative: www.level3creative.com

ISBN: 978-1-326-18538-1

*This is for Angelica and Joe*
*– my two co-pilots!*

# Table of Contents

# The Author

Mark Hillary is a British author, blogger, and advisor on the Internet, technology and globalization. His areas of business expertise involve publishing, technology, and social media.

He has written several successful books, including 'Global Services: Moving to a Level Playing Field', 'Who Moved My Job?', 'Talking Outsourcing', and 'Building a Future with BRICs'. The United Nations, the British Computer Society, Viva books, and the well-respected academic publisher, Springer, have all published Mark's work.

His most recent book, 'Reality Check: Life in Brazil through the eyes of a foreigner', explored his move to Brazil and reached the #1 chart position for books about Brazil written in English. The British Consul-General in Brazil, Richard Turner, even contributed a foreword to the book.

Based in São Paulo, Brazil, Mark is the co-founder of Carnaby. The company is focused on advice and social media content creation and translation for companies and works with clients in Brazil, the USA, Europe, Asia, and Africa.

As one of the best-known technology and globalization bloggers in the world today, Mark regularly contributes to The Huffington Post and his journalism has been published by the BBC, Financial Times, Reuters, and Computer Weekly.

Mark was one of the official British bloggers covering the London 2012 Olympics. He was shortlisted as business blogger of the year in 2009 and 2011 by Computer Weekly and won the SSON 2011 best blogger award.

Other work Mark has done in recent years include projects with the UN on the development of the IT industry in Africa and Bangladesh, the Indian government on service exports, and the British government on developing a hi-tech economy – as well as being a blogging mentor to teenage children under the guidance of the UK Department for Education.

Until his move to Brazil in 2010, Mark spent seven years as a visiting MBA lecturer at London South Bank University, focused on corporate structures and the globalization of services. He has lectured at several other universities, including the London School of Economics and the University of Loughborough.

The BBC reported Mark's wedding to Angelica in 2010 because they organized the entire event using social networks. You can view the BBC News report here:

*http://j.mp/hillarywedding*

Mark is currently on the public diplomacy committee of the British Ambassador to Brazil, focused on working with British artists to promote business and tourism to the UK.

*Photo of Mark Hillary by qhphotography.com*

**www.facebook.com/markhillarybooks**
**www.markhillary.com**
**@markhillary**

# Preface

In October 2014, online technology journal *The Next Web* ran a feature[1] on content marketing trends with a sub-heading that read:

"Director of content" is the new highly recruited marketing title".

Forget about the strained use of English. Of course, it might just be easier to just say that this is a newly popular job title, rather than suggesting that it is now "highly recruited", but the point is clear: people involved in marketing are exploring how content can help them, more than ever before.

I believe that what we are now witnessing is not just an explosion in new types of marketing, or new activities for marketing managers. We are witnessing a fundamental change in the way that people communicate.

Language and writing have always evolved. Think of the way a nineteenth century novelist might take an entire page or two to describe a room. A modern writer would probably just use a simile – 'the room looked like a dog kennel' – and then allow the reader to work it out with their imagination.

Spoken language has also been influenced by the devices we use to communicate. In the nineties, txtspk abbreviations evolved with dropped vowels to save space on SMS text messages, a style that has been making a comeback with the forced brevity of Twitter.

But think more generally about all forms of communication and contact with others. How do you communicate today? Think about the way that people engage with politicians, find a new partner using online dating, educate themselves at a university halfway around the world, work for a boss in a different country, or transfer money without even talking to their bank.

To say that our media and sources of news and information are also changing is an understatement.

A third of American adults now use Facebook as their primary news source[2]. This doesn't mean that they only pay attention to cat videos: every media brand pushes their news into Facebook.

But there is so much information that could be displayed that a Facebook algorithm now selects what you see on your timeline to avoid it just becoming a fire hose of photos and adverts. For many people, social network algorithms are now deciding what news they see and what they don't.

The way we receive information about companies, products, and services is changing just as quickly as all these other aspects of our lives. Yet, as the formal and established news channels have moved from the printed page to the online environment, there has also been a blurring of where news originates.

News, research and information from blogs can all be featured on Facebook newsfeeds and Twitter timelines without first being published in more established media outlets. People are using social networks as a way of curating the subjects they are interested in – and then only ever seeing news on those subjects.

When Captain 'Sully' Sullenberger landed US Airways Flight 1549 safely in the Hudson river after suffering a bird strike during take-off from New York's La Guardia airport on January 15$^{th}$ 2009, this was already being discussed on Twitter within four minutes[3]. Traditional media outlets took another 15 minutes before they mentioned that a plane carrying 155 passengers and crew had taken off in New York and almost immediately crash-landed into the river.

The photographs and eyewitness commentary about this event were shared on Twitter thousands of times in that 15-minute period before professional journalists took over.

The way we find information and how that has changed in our personal lives also applies to the world of business. Over-loaded people are getting smarter about how to deal with the deluge of information that hits them each day. Curation and filtering is now normal even if you don't use these terms.

With this book I wanted to create a short, sharp focus on the world of executive blogging. I've been involved in this type of work directly for almost a decade now and although it still feels very new to many executives the BBC's technology correspondent, Rory Cellan-Jones[4], documented this type of content creation when he interviewed me for the Radio 4 Today program way back in 2008.

At that time, we were still trying to cope with the growth of the major social networks and smart phones were not yet ubiquitous. All this has now changed.

Executives and marketing teams need to devise completely new ways to reach influencers in their industry and the use of content and social media is a very powerful strategy. But it remains a path that many companies have attempted and few are getting right.

In this book I will explore how it works, how it fails, and how to make the most of content rather than just falling into the trap of creating a social media program that achieves little more than elevating the Klout score of your CEO.

This book is not long. Unfortunately, I meet more and more people today who don't read any books at all. It is certain that in the business world nobody reads long books, so I have tried getting to the point quickly and I hope you appreciate my brevity. I consider it respectful to the reader to just get to the point – if only more business and management writers could take this approach.

I would briefly like to thank everyone that has helped me to produce this book. I conceived the idea early in 2014 and wrote a Huffington Post article summarizing my views (see Appendix E). The main work on the book took place in mid-2014 followed by a few months where I was travelling too much to complete it. I therefore completed the book late in 2014 ready for release on New Year's Day 2015.

Many of my clients have been particularly helpful. They are the reason I have all these experiences to share. I can't name them all as I deliberately wrote this book with anonymous observations on how different companies have behaved, however they know who they are and should get in touch – we are probably overdue a drink together if it is a former client.

Peter Ryan at Ovum and Stephen Loynd at Frost & Sullivan are two industry analysts that I often share ideas – and jokes – with. I'm grateful to these guys for their observations on how customer service is changing. If you follow us all on Twitter then you can join in on some of the discussions – and jokes... @peter_w_ryan and @loyndsview.

Sean Cook at Level 3 Creative in the UK designed the cover for the book. Sean and I go way back to our teenage years working in a supermarket together. Now he runs a graphic design company and I'm writing books in Brazil – life changes fast.

*www.level3creative.com*

I asked friends on my Facebook page (facebook.com/markhillarybooks) if they could suggest a title for this book and I received dozens of ideas. The best one was very close to what I settled on eventually - and was suggested by Gaby Castro-Fontoura. Thanks for the idea Gaby!

*www.twitter.com/uklatinamerica*

I started this book in Santos, São Paulo, and completed it in Serra Negra – also in São Paulo state. Thanks to the power of modern publishing platforms it will be seen globally even as I commence work on the next book.

My deepest thanks go out to my wife Angelica. She is a published author herself so she knows the effort that goes into each book – even the short ones! She is also a great source of inspiration for me as she regularly launches a new social campaign or toys with a new business idea. Thank you for your patience Angie…!

Please do reach out and let me know what you think using one of the networks suggested here:

**www.facebook.com/markhillarybooks**

**www.markhillary.com**

**@markhillary**

# Chapter 1: Introduction

There are many books - and blogs - about the process of blogging. I appreciate this more than most as I have spent long enough searching for pearls of wisdom myself. And I also know that this is a world populated with plenty of charlatans and self-proclaimed social media "gurus."

I am not a marketing or public relations practitioner or graduate – although one of my publishers did once call me a "guru" without asking if I wanted that on the book cover! For a business to be seen blogging is a marketing exercise, but it should also be seen within the context of how the communications function has changed in the past decade. Blogging is no longer something new to be feared, it is how most of us obtain our information on a daily basis, even if we are not aware of it.

Therefore, whatever type of business you are in, if you want customers or potential customers to know what you are offering, you need to be engaging with the media that most people are consuming.

This book is mainly concerned with the Business-to-Business (B2B) environment, meaning companies that need to sell to other companies rather than individual consumers (B2C). My own experience is with these companies and everything within this book is based on my own work history, not just the marketing textbooks I read when I studied for my MBA at Liverpool.

I'm not going to explore Search Engine Optimization (SEO) in much depth here. SEO is important if you want your content to be noticed, but in the B2B world audiences are smaller anyway. It's easier to focus on a small and highly relevant audience using tools such as LinkedIn, when the company creating the content operates in the B2B environment. A B2C blogging strategy would certainly have a greater requirement for good SEO – the corporate website is generally more important for these brands.

The B2B environment is where there is more of a need for good advice and comment. Most executives in B2B organizations know their market and potential customers already; it may even be a very small audience. These are the people who often need convincing to move beyond collegiate lunches with prospects into the world of social media.

Businesses that sell their products direct to consumers will communicate in a different way to those needing to convince other businesses to buy their products. For example, as I write this page, I can see the Coca Cola Twitter feed (@cocacola) featuring videos of surprised football legends being handed the actual FIFA World Cup™ Trophy.

Consumer marketing is clearly more related to branding and the creation of a psychological attachment, or affection, for a product. I might share a video of a Ford car on my personal social networks because I identify with the scenario presented or I might 'like' a video by Nike because I'm a fan of the athlete in the campaign.

None of this really applies to the B2B world. Some brands do use celebrities and branding to create knowledge of what they do, but in terms of what we are trying to achieve when blogging, it is almost useless to try creating a brand using a blog, what we want is to demonstrate knowledge of the market and competence in what the company does and then use that to engage with the key market influencers.

But before I get started, it's important to see where and how this book originated so you can understand why I am writing this now. In addition, the first chapter of this book will explore the importance of blogging more generally, how it has become an important part of how we all gather information about the world – what we used to call 'the news'.

To complete this introduction, you will need to indulge me a few paragraphs of my own work history because it helps to place what I am doing today in context.

I studied computer science and software engineering and I started my career as a professional computer programmer. My first real job with a monthly salary was developing software for retail point-of-sale systems. I coded the software that checked credit cards for the Tesco supermarket chain and did similar work for the Dixons electrical stores in the UK.

I moved from retail to banking technology and got a job on a trading floor in the City of London. I was still a technology guy, but then I was in the middle of one of those trading floors where people operated three phones and six computers all at the same time. My job was to build systems that let them keep track of what they were trading and to try building new systems that might identify trading opportunities – one of my projects at the time was codenamed 'Bonanza'.

I moved from the first bank I worked in to a banking software start-up – a big mistake as I nearly burned out from the stress – but eventually went back to a major investment bank in an analysis role, where I designed the equity (shares) trading systems used by the bank globally.

I rose up the ranks over time to the point where I managed all of the equity trading technology systems used by the bank - all over the world. I managed support teams on every trading floor, software development in Singapore and India, as well as analysts in all the major trading centers around the world.

I played an instrumental role in helping the bank create a large technology delivery function in Bengaluru (formerly Bangalore) and I spent a lot of time working in India and exploring the concepts of offshore outsourcing – I was asking colleagues and peers why companies are doing this and who is doing it well?

I wrote a book about the experience of going to India ('Outsourcing to India: The Offshore Advantage', Springer 2004) and though I moved on from that job to head the European technology function in another bank, the writing bug bit me.

I quit and started focusing on writing another book and editorial work for the business press. It was a big career change, but my books were well received and allowed me to work as a consultant to many companies – a far more diverse and interesting experience than my time in the various banks.

Although I had been blogging on LiveJournal since the early days of that platform, it was only once I started writing professionally that I became a more serious blogger. I started a regular blog in the British technology magazine *Computing* focused on businesses that were outsourcing and this ran for several years and resulted in a book-of-the-blog called *Talking Outsourcing* – published in 2009.

I followed *Computing* editor Bryan Glick as he moved on to *Computer Weekly* magazine and continued to write a regular blog for him, but by that time my focus had shifted more towards the corporate use of social media.

With all this exposure from books about technology and blogs in some of the leading UK business technology journals, I was often asked to help companies with their own ideas around blogging – in particular when companies wanted their senior executives to be seen blogging.

And so I found that company executives within the technology and hi-tech service companies would pay me to be their ghost blogger. They already had marketing agencies and PR agencies (Public Relations) and various other kinds of communication support, but none of this helped very much when trying to write in the voice of the executive.

Most people find it hard to write, even senior executives who are good at what they do. Thinking of an argument, introducing it, arguing a point, then summarizing it for the reader all comes naturally to a journalist. But if you are not a professional writer it can take a very long time to come up with even 200 words that read well on a blog – let alone a more detailed, 1,000-word article.

The executives that approached me did not want a marketing professional writing their blogs. They could not afford the time to personally write their content, but they could spare some time to give their ideas to a writer and have their thoughts translated into compelling content. They wanted someone who could write, but who also had some industry experience, a person who knew what it was like to be on the road all the time, or making decisions that affect people's career – or bonus.

So that's how all of this started for me. I have advised on blogs and social media and ghosted for chief executives in companies on five continents for the past nine years.

I have also drafted speeches about technology for ambassadors, toured the UK talking to schoolchildren about future careers on behalf of the British government, and helped Neil Armstrong add some jokes about IT and telecoms to his standard Apollo 11 speech just before he gave a talk to 3,500 telecoms salespeople in Las Vegas.

In short, I have found that people started considering me an expert on blogging and social media not because I blogged more frequently than anyone else, but because I had experience as an executive and could also write – I accidentally developed this niche as a blogger through my management experience.

Which leads me back to this book. This brief résumé of my career to date is included just to emphasize that I have written hundreds of thousands of words for senior managers all over the world and my experience of what works and doesn't work is recorded here. I'm not going to name names or companies, but rest assured that when I give examples of what really doesn't work, it's because I've had to experience that pain personally.

# Chapter 2: Blogging Becomes Content Marketing

Blogging is no longer what it once was. A blogger today is a critical part of the media and news infrastructure that we once trusted to newspapers and the TV news channels. Blogs are now where almost all of our news originates because they allow instantaneous publishing by anyone.

If this sounds too bold a claim then look back at the news you have viewed today. Of course there are still widely respected media organizations, such as the BBC or New York Times, which have a strong editorial team, but look again at the 'others'. How many 'news' stories now originated from little more than a YouTube video or a photo on Instagram?

This universal ability to publish has led to the creation of blogging celebrities, such as Perez Hilton. Perez specializes in swapping gossip about celebrities. This might not seem like the bedrock of our present-day news industry, but there has been an entire change in how we receive and process information in the past decade.

In the 2011 movie 'Contagion', directed by Steven Soderbergh, the actor Jude Law plays a professional blogger. At one point in the film his character is abused with the line: *"Blogging is just graffiti with punctuation!"*

A lot has changed since the early days of blogging. Both our consumption of news and information has changed as well as the way this information is created. To understand how blogs work it is important to have an understanding of both these processes.

## How we read

How did you get your news today? Did you take a walk this morning to a store, pick up the same newspaper you have purchased for years, then take it home or to your place of work and sit consuming it page by page?

I doubt it. News consumption has changed dramatically in the past few decades and has been even more rapidly changed in the past five to ten years.

Neil Postman's classic book analyzing the media, "Amusing ourselves to death," documents the shift from a print-based media to television in the 1980s. Postman made the point that news has become entertainment with attractive presenters and dramatic music before and after bulletins.

It could be argued that news on TV has always been presented this way, but it has certainly deteriorated since the 1980s as documented by Postman, with the increasingly explicit partisan nature of TV news as most visibly demonstrated by Fox News in the US[1].

In March 2014, the Washington Post conducted a national survey of Americans to ask what action they believe the US government should take against Russia because of their invasion of the Crimean peninsula in Ukraine. The respondents were also asked to locate Ukraine on a map of the world.

The survey results showed that there was a strong correlation between those who encouraged military action or some form of intervention by the US government and those who actually have no idea where Ukraine is[2].

People have an opinion because they hear about 'the news' and yet they have little underlying knowledge of the issues involved, particularly in complex geopolitical situations. A good example would be the ongoing (just about) campaigns in Afghanistan and Iraq since 2003.

Most people have long forgotten why the US and their allies ever went into these countries and this culture of disinformation is why the former Iraqi leader Saddam Hussein's name is still connected to the 9/11 New York terrorist attacks.

But even if you talk to someone who does have an interest in following the TV news and claims to have a deep knowledge of international affairs based on their news consumption, asking a question such as 'what is the most commonly spoken language in Afghanistan' will often be enough to throw them.

That is because even if the media reports world events, it is in a way that entertains rather than informs. Bite. Sized. Chunks.

But let's move on from the TV news. It is increasingly common to not read a single journal or to watch traditional broadcast news at all: instead, we can browse everything we are interested in, all at the same time.

The combination of social networks, like Facebook and Twitter, now allow us to follow only those subjects or people we are interested in. This creates a content stream that is partly updated by our personal friends, partly by celebrities, and partly by brands. I can look at my Facebook news stream in the morning and see what my friends are doing, how

Russell Crowe looked at his latest movie premiere and how the Chilean people are dealing with the latest earthquake in their country. It truly is my news feed.

Now combine this with the smartphone revolution experienced since the launch of the Apple iPhone in 2007 and there is a potent mix. Many people never tune into a news broadcast or purchase a newspaper – ever. They can follow everything on Facebook, Twitter or other social networking channels. The news comes to the individual without them having to find it by tuning into a specific channel at a specific time.

News bulletins at fixed times already feel quaint, even archaic to many people. However, there are some examples of rolling news stories where the constant need for endless news updates can stretch the patience of the viewer and a more authoritative update would feel more appropriate. Good examples of this are news stories such as the mysterious vanishing aircraft in 2014. When MH370 and QZ8501 went missing the journalists were drowning in a frenzy of opinion, but nobody had any knowledge of what had really happened, so speculation filled the void – for MH370 it still does.

News that is 'liked' can be shared or forwarded, so your choice of friends is now far more influential than any specific journal or news channel that you might browse from time to time.

There has been a blurring of communication channels. I never used to watch the TV news for information about the party my friends went to last night, but this is how social networks represent our information. Personal updates are mixed with news supplied by professional journalists mixed with commentary from bloggers mixed with updates from brands such as Guinness, Nike, and Coca Cola. We now consume all this information as a single stream of updates that are all of interest to us, regardless of the original source.

# How news is created

It is not just how we consume the news that has changed over the past decade, but also the way it is created.

The environment used to be fairly simple and hierarchical. At the top of the tree were the big broadcast news bulletins, the early evening 6pm news on the BBC being a good example – a flagship show – 'the six' - that hundreds of staff would work on each day. These reports were authoritative and reliable.

Below the big broadcast shows there would be the regional channels and in print, you had the national newspapers sitting above the regional and trade titles.

Stories could bubble between the various types of news outlet, for instance if a technology journal had a scoop about a failed government IT project then the exclusive would probably run first in the trade journal and it would then be followed up by national print or broadcast journalists.

And this is the important point to remember: only journalists or other newsgathering professionals were involved in the creation of these newspaper and TV news bulletins, regardless of how stories bubbled around the various outlets.

Now we have blogs added to the mix. Niche blogs that focus on a single topic in great detail and general blogs that get more readers than established journals.

The Huffington Post is a good example[3]. Their audience is enormous, with the site regularly located in the top three news sources in the world today. Yet most of the contributors are not paid. They are bloggers, not professional journalists.

This has been controversial. How can the content be any good if nobody is paid? The Huffington Post strategy was to get subject matter experts to blog news and opinion directly. Why get a crime reporter to synthesize a story together featuring comment from several legal experts when you could just get a contribution from the experts directly? Those experts write for free because it boosts their professional profile in their own industry network.

Naturally, there are many professional journalists who think that The Huffington Post is the work of the Devil.

But, anybody can start a blog. There is no cost involved, unless you want to pay a bit extra to make your blog look better than the standard tools allow. Even a highly professional looking blog can be created for a very small investment.

When I first moved to São Paulo, I started blogging about the technology industry in Brazil. My wife is an experienced technology journalist and between us we would make sure there was something new on the site every day. Within a few months we were getting around 10,000 readers every single day – without a marketing budget or any of the costs associated with launching a traditional magazine.

Most of our traffic came from Google News. Google was including our blogs in their news search results alongside stories from long-established media companies.

This democratization of access to 'the news' has allowed citizens to enter the world of journalism, contributing their videos and photos to the established media when they witness a major event and capture it on their smart phone camera – just like the plane landing in a river in New York that I mentioned earlier.

Regular citizens with no training in journalism can contribute to the traditional media or just create their own journals or video channels. The actor and comedian Russell Brand[4] has demonstrated by creating his *'The Trews'* (true news) video news channel on YouTube in 2014. Brand has become a serious – though controversial - political commentator just by uploading his opinion to YouTube.

The 'blogosphere', as some still call it, has become a feeder channel into the traditional news outlets. How many stories have you seen recently in established media outlets – print or broadcast – that are basically a story about a piece of content a member of the public has uploaded?

Car crashes on YouTube, lucky escapes, celebrities photographed shopping in the supermarket, all of these examples of citizen journalism commonly cross over to the regular journals. The traditional journals and even broadcast news shows now trawl the blogs looking for interesting content to share on their own outlets.

Nowhere is this more evident than on the Daily Mail website. This traditional British newspaper created an online presence that bears almost no resemblance to their paper edition. The online version is filled with banal celebrity 'news' that should really be of no interest to anyone. A look at the Daily Mail today tells me that actor Jonah Hill has put on some weight recently, Kourtney Kardashian walked past a convenience store on the way to meet her sister, and singer Rihanna may or may not be pregnant. True news indeed.

This celebrity trash and the photographs of celebrities snapped by the public should not really be news, but all of this does generate clicks. People click on the stories to read all this gossip and with 190 million unique readers each month, who could argue that the Daily Mail is wrong?[5]

We exist in an undefined media universe at present. Print journals were financed by a cover price and advertising. Broadcast news was paid for by advertising – or by some form of tax, such as a license fee. With blogs and online news there remains ongoing confusion about how it will all be paid for.

The two opposing schools of thought can be best summarized as the free-for-all model, with the Daily Mail as a good example. By giving away all their news for free, the Daily Mail encourages more sharing and more readers and therefore can charge advertisers a commensurate rate to reach that large audience.

Others in the industry, such as News International boss Rupert Murdoch, are attempting to enforce paid access to their news through the use of paywalls – restrictions on access to their new sites without a subscription.

I don't believe that either side will win this argument. I fully expect one of the technology industry giants such as Google or Facebook to create an open micro-payment mechanism where I can pay for the media I consume on a per-story basis.

The Blendle app does this already in the Netherlands, but to go completely global it will require an enormous existing network – probably only Facebook or Google at present - and the ability to incorporate a reliable payment system.

What is important to remember though is that blogs and citizen content have not only become a feeder into the traditional media brands, they are spurring these news organizations into new types of behavior too. Citizens usually get stories – and publish them - before journalists today.

When the singer Michael Jackson died in 2009, the TMZ blog featured the news at least half an hour before any other news outlet causing the Internet to explode in a frenzy of people checking to see if it was true or just another one of those 'celebrity death' Internet rumors that high school students start for fun.

TMZ managed to achieve this by having contacts all over Los Angeles reporting gossip back to the site. We can safely assume that many of these people are in privileged positions, in hospitals or police stations, and probably are rewarded for their tip-offs. I don't know the exact operating procedure or *modus operandi*, but let's just assume that anyone with good information is going to be rewarded.

But learning about the death of a singer half an hour earlier than the rest of world sounds trivial. Is it really that important to accelerate our lives even further?

Unfortunately, this is important because traditional news outlets don't want to be last to publish a story. They are under pressure to be seen setting the news agenda and therefore the content published on blogs is not only feeding into what they publish, it is encouraging them to publish sooner, with fewer facts checked than ever before.

In his book "Trust me I'm lying," Ryan Holiday, the former marketing director of clothing brand American Apparel, describes how easy it is to feed false news stories to blogs and to then watch them bubble into trusted news outlets. Because the professional journalists don't want to be seen as late to the story they often run stories from blogs without checking sources in the way a traditional story would be fact-checked.

An excellent example of this is how Mohammed Islam, a 17-year-old student in New York, told a magazine reporter that he had earned $72 million trading stocks during his lunch break at school. The story was repeated across the world with the New York Post even reporting the story as front-page news. He just made up the story and the first reporter didn't check; subsequent reporters trusted the story[6]. If it's published somewhere then it has to be true.

We really are now in a world where blogs and traditional news journals are indistinguishable from each other.

## How does all this turn into marketing for my business?

This change in the way we consume news is all very interesting for media students, but you might be asking how it helps you to promote your business. There are a couple of key points to remember from what you have just read:

- Blog content can easily bubble into the traditional media agenda;
- Blogs and corporate content are now included in news streams along with other content of interest to specific readers.

This change in the way that information is consumed has created the possibility for content to be used for marketing. Instead of a company publishing information as press releases, product announcements, or other news that is specific to what the company is doing, the company can also attract interest from prospective customers just by talking more generally about the industry they are engaged in.

In his book "The Curve," Nicholas Lovell gives the example of River Pools, a swimming pool sales and maintenance company that serves the Virginia and Maryland area of the USA[7]. River Pools used to spend $250,000 a year advertising on the radio and on pay-per-click web adverts until the company founder Marcus Sheridan had an epiphany.

He figured that when most people want information about swimming pools, they go to the Internet and use a search engine to ask questions. He was already using tools like Google Adwords so his ads would appear when potential customers were searching for relevant topics, but he wondered whether he could just start publishing some common questions and answers  - would these answers start popping up in the search engine results automatically if customers were searching for answers to these common problems?

He wrote blog posts answering those common questions, comparing his company to the competition, and even openly debating the pros and cons of fiberglass swimming pools – the product his company is primarily focused on. This change in approach took place in 2009 and in the past five years Sheridan estimates that his initial blog post has generated over $1.7 million in new business.

Because now whenever anyone searches online for information on swimming pools, particularly fiberglass pools, it is Sheridan's company that comes top of the search results – organically. They find that customers will often get in touch for an appointment and they have read thirty or more pages of his blogs about swimming pools. Prospective clients like this are much easier to turn into sales than those who just clicked on an advert – they are interested in the content before they even get in touch to discuss a possible purchase.

We have moved on from just calling this process "corporate blogging." Now we are referring to the process of publishing corporate information, which is not specifically advertising, as content marketing.

We are telling stories, providing information on products and services by talking about the issues rather than hard-selling the solutions.

The Content Marketing Institute[8] defines content marketing as:

> *"Content marketing is a marketing technique of creating and distributing valuable, relevant and consistent content to attract and acquire a clearly defined audience – with the objective of driving profitable customer action."*

The institute goes on to add:

*"Content marketing's purpose is to attract and retain customers by consistently **creating and curating relevant and valuable content** with the **intention of changing** or enhancing **consumer behaviour**. It is an **ongoing process** that is best integrated into your overall marketing strategy, and it focuses on **owning media**, not renting it."*

Then the next paragraph in their definition is what I would declare the kicker that nails it:

*"Basically, content marketing is the art of communicating with your customers and prospects without selling. It is non-interruption marketing. Instead of\ pitching your products or services, you are delivering information that makes your buyer more intelligent. The essence of this content strategy is the belief that if we, as businesses, deliver consistent, ongoing valuable information to buyers, they ultimately reward us with their business and loyalty."*

If you can communicate with your customers and prospects and show that you are the best at what you do without just pitching or advertising then this makes your buyer more intelligent and more likely to work with your company.

In the case or River Pools there is a high value product that customers will want to research extensively before buying, allowing them to build a freely available online resource that can draw customers to their business.

In the case of a common consumer product, like Coca Cola, this would not work so well. Coke is sold because people want a cold soft drink and given the choice of various drinks the customer chooses Coke mainly because they identify with the brand – many brands of drink are equally tasty and can be served just as cold. If the Coca Cola Company published details of their expertise in making beverages it would probably appeal to very few actual consumers of the product.

But this is why content marketing is such a powerful tool for companies that operate in a B2B environment, only ever selling to managers in other companies. This is an audience that really does want to understand your expertise and ability to deliver.

The power of content marketing for the B2B audience extends much further than just the ability to create a body of work proclaiming your expertise in a given business area. Most B2B purchasing decisions are taken by managers after consulting with information available in the marketplace; before one company buys from another they might read a consultant's report, information published by an industry analyst, or even the view of a business journalist.

These influencers are the real targets for a B2B content marketing campaign. If you can demonstrate knowledge of your industry in a way that impresses the journalists who write about your sector, or the industry analysts who compare your company to your competitors, or the consultants who advise your clients which company they should do business with, then you are not just blogging. You are building relationships with the people who influence your customers.

This engagement is what is truly valuable, but it would be hard to achieve without using content on a blog to establish your credibility and knowledge.

# Chapter 3: My Own Experience; The Good, The Bad, and The Ugly

As I mentioned in the introduction, I have personally had experience of many different types of content marketing campaigns. Most of the B2B clients I have worked are drawn from the hi-tech IT or IT-related industries, such as services delivered using IT, however this has broadened in recent years with clients also including telcos, customer service experts and lawyers.

Regardless of the industry you work with, these examples of previous clients are relevant as they describe how the B2B organization and content producer need to work together - this applies in the same way to companies in any industry.

Later on in the book, I will list more explicitly how to make a ghostwriting relationship work and how it can fail, but these are some of the environments I have worked in.

## Client One: "The Management Consultant."

A friend of mine introduced me to the head of the consulting group in this big global IT Company. He was a smart operator who believed that the company could be getting more business in general consulting, the kind of advisory work that firms like Accenture or KPMG seem to always win based on their reputation alone.

He set me to work churning out thought leadership papers that would be published in the name of various consultants in the group, but I soon ran into two problems.

1. **My style was wrong for them.** I was writing with business journals such as The Economist and Financial Times as my style guides – clear and simple English, but with the ability to describe complex topics. These guys wanted me to use a kind of overt 'management' style with buzzwords and jargon, as regularly mocked in most of the business press. I once loaded a paper with as many business buzzwords as I could possibly think of – and they loved it.
2. **They couldn't deliver most of what I was writing about; so many of the papers I wrote were never published.** This was natural to me because I had been asked to think into the future and talk about where various industries are headed, but when I wrote about something they could not sell, the consultants were not interested in using the papers. So much for thought leadership.

## The shift to ghostwriting

Fortunately, one of the consultants was launching an expensive spin-off to the business – an innovation lab. This would be a real physical lab where cutting edge technologies could be tested on real-life problems.

I had suggested a blog to support the activities of the lab and I was soon ghostwriting blogs on behalf of the innovation lab director.

This was a great assignment for a number of reasons. I got on well with the director and I thought he was a smart guy who didn't want anything in his name to be full of buzzwords. He had some genuine ideas about where things were headed in his industry beyond just fighting fires today and pitching clients for more business – it was exciting to be there trying to document his ideas.

But this project eventually failed, because it was too much of a *skunk works* initiative for the management of the company in Asia. The writing was on the wall when someone in the communications department of the head office noticed all these popular blogs and asked how they could see all this material online, when it had not been cleared by the head office.

The lab director told them that he had permission to publish material that promoted his work and that's exactly what he was doing. Their response was that they had not expected him to be publishing globally – a fundamental disconnect with the way the Internet works.

I managed to continue with them for a while, but the face of innovation in the company was switched to be the Chief Information Officer (CIO), who was based in Mumbai. I met him a few times and I could see that he was a clever guy, but he didn't really understand how to communicate using a blog. When he wrote content himself it was long and full of technical information, demonstrating his credentials, but hardly drawing an audience.

This contract died a slow death, but as they were paying me on a daily basis I kept on going with whatever they wanted me to do until they eventually transferred the ghostwriting to a junior public relations officer in India who would basically just write whatever was dictated by the CIO.

A couple of additional memories of this company linger with me and though not directly related to the experience of blogging for them, they do give an insight into the way some multi-billion dollar companies organize their communications.

Although the company was (and remains) focused on IT, their global PR contract was with a firm that had no real experience or track record in technology. To put it mildly, they were rubbish and almost certainly chosen because of executives in different companies who knew each other. Golf course contracts, I guess.

When I first arrived on the scene with the consulting team, the head of consulting asked me how he could get some more attention from the media. I said that he could do some specialized PR, reaching out to journalists that would be interested in what he was doing – and, as much of his work was advising the British government, it should be easy to get him some media appearances.

I suggested a PR firm run by a friend of mine, not just because he was a mate, but because it was exactly the kind of guerrilla-style marketing campaign they specialize in – getting companies noticed when they have been ignored for ages.

I was granted a £10,000 budget just to see what happens – not much at all. It was only supposed to last a couple of months and then we would review if it were worth investing more. Within the first few days of activity the consulting head had been on the prestigious BBC Today Radio 4 show and had made a couple of TV news appearances – he was in demand.

Unfortunately, when the communications team in Mumbai heard about all his media appearances, they told him to stop it. Apparently, thinking for yourself and getting the company noticed is not allowed if it has not been planned from the head office.

After I had left the client, their UK head of communications called me to say she had been given an enormous amount of cash to place a full page advert in the Financial Times newspaper, so she wanted my opinion on the best page to place the advert.

I said that for the same amount of money I could run a blogging campaign for over a year that would generate an enormous amount of content in the name of the company executives, get them noticed, and allow them to engage with influencers.

But she said that the money could only be used for a newspaper advert – which nobody ever noticed and was just used to wrap proverbial fish and chips a day later.

## *Project Summary*

Intention: The client wanted to promote their ability to deliver innovation from a lab environment by using innovative communication tools, rather than the traditional PR and advertising led methods.

Issues: Although the business team was measured on their ability to interest clients in pilot tests of new innovations, the communications team was remunerated using traditional methods and measured from an overseas head office. This meant that the business team found it very difficult to move beyond any traditional forms of communication.

Alternatives: The business team should have been able to co-opt some of the communication budget or the communication team should have been able to align their own success more tightly with the objectives of the business team.

## Client Two: "The Back-Office Experts."

This European company was mainly focused on government Business Process Outsourcing (BPO) work, but also did a lot of IT Outsourcing (ITO) so they were a bit of an all-rounder, which works for some projects, but can also mean they get a bit of a reputation for being a 'Jack of all trades and master of none.'

Nonetheless, we had eased into a relationship over a period of a few years. I attend a lot of industry conferences and they started asking me to blog for them on their corporate website using a very simple payment structure – find and interview people at big IT conferences and they would pay me per interview.

This meant that I had some very busy conferences when I knew I was working for them, as I would loiter around the stage after every speech trying to get a quick comment from the speaker. Each blog meant more cash for me.

After a few years of this sporadic content production, they suggested that we create something ongoing that would set them apart in the marketplace. I was asked to act as editor and writer for a new blog they would run on their corporate website as a big information exchange between their team and others in the same industry.

I was blogging for a couple of their senior managers, but I was mainly editing contributions from others. I had a budget to commission contributions from journalists and I was chasing their internal team from all over the world, asking for contributions to the blog.

This was a very active and imaginative blog. We had some great content from good writers and there was a steady stream of information from inside the company.

This could have been developed further, but the entire project was eventually shelved because of the global economic slowdown. When companies want to cut their spending quickly then marketing and other areas seen as non-essential to making quick sales are often the victims.

With hindsight, the project could have been continued at a much lower cost. All the external journalist budget could have been canned immediately and I could have even lowered my rate as a goodwill gesture to keep the project running, but so many corporate decisions veer between black and white – we are either going to spend a lot on marketing or we are going to fire the marketing director and spend nothing.

## *Project Summary*

Intention: The communications team wanted to publish industry opinion on their own site that could bubble into the trade press – demonstrating their ability to think differently about solutions when compared to the competition.

Issues: The 2008 economic crash was the biggest issue here as it destroyed any willingness to invest in long-term marketing programs that might not produce instant rewards. However, a further issue was that this was really a company creating an industry magazine, with an editor and journalists creating content editorially independent of the sponsor.

This can be a very powerful content marketing strategy, but the marketing and communications team at this company did not want to let go of editorial control to the extent that it could be a semi-independent magazine and that left it with an uncertain position – corporate blog or industry comment?

Alternatives: With a similar budget, but a little more editorial freedom this project could have developed into a very focused niche journal that would highlight the work of the sponsor in addition to providing more general industry comment. Even when the economic crash hit, with a little thought it could have been populated by more content from inside the company, which would have reduced the external writer budget and allowed much of the momentum to have been maintained.

## Client Three: "The Debt-Collectors."

I was invited to participate in a project with a large American Business Process Outsourcing (BPO) firm involved mainly in work such as collections and credit card bill processing. The invitation was from a PR agency I knew –

they had won the communications contract with the client and promised a social media element to the contract, but nobody in the agency knew about blogging so they subcontracted all that to me.

It was clear from early on that the social media element of the contract had not been described very well. I was brought in after the terms and conditions had been agreed between the client and the PR agency who were sub-contracting social media and blog related work to my firm.

The scope of my part of the contract was to specifically provide ghostwriting services to the Chief Executive. It was no problem for me or for him – we met and liked each other. He gave me some ideas and made himself available for calls now and then so I was always able to find out what he wanted to say on certain subjects and the areas he was keen to be seen talking about.

But the communications structure within the company meant that nothing could be issued in the name of the Chief Executive Officer (CEO) without it being subject to a number of procedures first.

I would submit my draft blog to the British communications head, who would check it and submit it to the head office communications team who would check it and then submit it to the CEO in person. There was no delegation of responsibility and even when the CEO himself said that he wanted people on the team to take responsibility they would still forward it to him anyway - 'just for checking.'

In the six months I was writing for this client, I believe that only one blog was ever published, but I was on a fixed monthly retainer so I was getting paid even though I was tearing my hair out at the lack of publication. Getting paid to do nothing might seem ideal, but it's not a long-term strategy for success.

## *Project Summary*

Intention: The CEO was keen to be seen blogging and commenting on the industry with timely and relevant views about industry issues.

Issues: The culture of the organization did not allow anyone to sign off on the 'words of the CEO' without the CEO personally approving them – even when the CEO insisted that he wanted the communications team to start doing this they feared his reaction to any mistakes. Therefore a bottleneck existed which made it impossible for any timely communications to come from the CEO, or any other senior executive.

Alternatives: It is easy to suggest that the CEO should have worked harder to delegate responsibility when the culture of the company was clearly to live in fear of ever making a mistake, but this is the bottom line. The CEO should have devised a more streamlined decision-making process for all communications before adding the blog to their responsibilities. The new process would also include protection for team members who make minor errors, while protecting the need to control messages from the CEO.

## Client Four: "The Contact Center Experts."

I once spent time attending several meetings and putting proposals together for the UK CEO of a big American BPO firm, which were all about trying to get this company online in a meaningful way.

None of it ever came to anything because the Americans running this company were from the pound-the-streets-knocking-on-doors school of sales, so they could see no benefit in giving the British CEO some visibility.

But when that boss moved on to a similar European firm he called me up and just said, "let's do it." I never had to pitch a new business plan or anything; he just wanted me to start ghostwriting a blog for him and his senior team and to help with the social media around that.

Over time, I spoke less and less to the CEO, who originally gave me the contract and had been happy to let his team appear on the blog far more than he did. But even so, he had appeared on various online lists of socially connected CEOs without him ever writing one of his own blogs.

Even though I spoke less to the CEO, I was still aware of where he was taking the business. I can't remember the last time I submitted a draft blog to him and received anything other than a green light to use the text – this was one of the more enjoyable clients to work with, because they just understand the process so well. I love working with companies like this.

The one downside was that we could do so much more together. I could focus more time and ideas just for them, but once a contract is in place and a price agreed, it's hard to significantly change it, even if the new ideas all sound great. Over the time we worked together I allowed the scope to expand, so I was doing more than ever originally agreed without earning more. But that was compensated by their loyalty as a client and many of the team felt more like personal friends.

## *Project Summary*

Intention: Initially the aim was to develop an online persona for the CEO by using blogs and social networks.

Issues: The main issue has been that the world of social media evolves so fast that the relationship needs to be flexible. What may be specified and contracted will not be what you are doing for the client in one year – both sides needed to grow with the environment in this example although it probably means that the legal contract is meaningless and the services are delivered in good faith rather than based on any legally contracted service levels.

Alternatives: This project demonstrates that it is a good idea to have an annual review of services required, allowing the ability to add new requirements, drop some that are less important, and review targets for the year ahead. The online environment moves fast and even an annual review may be too slow – what's better its to create a good relationship and an ability to be flexible with the services provided.

\*\*\*

Although all clients in the case studies listed here are B2B oriented and focus on a similar industry, they all functioned differently, with differing communication styles and corporate cultures. Later on in the book I will list specific guidance on what makes a blogging contract work and what makes it fail – in particular where ghosted content is a part of the deal.

# Chapter 4: Why is Social Media Important for B2B Firms?

D o you remember when social media really arrived, just over half a decade ago? It was feared by enterprises, in particular by corporate communication managers responsible for maintaining a cohesive brand image.

Managers banned Facebook access at work to prevent the scourge of employees wasting the day away on games like *Farmville* in much the same way we had to promise to not make personal calls from our desk phone, back in the eighties.

All this flies in the face of companies that are now trying to use blogging and social media in a positive way to help promote their brand. Take a look back at the document "Top 10 Corporate Social Media Predictions for 2012," published by advisory firm Useful Social Media[1].

The report picked ten executives responsible for social media strategy within their company and asked them what would be the most important change in 2012. It's a couple of years ago now, but most of the comments made by Jen McClure, the director of social media at news organization Thomson Reuters, still ring true:

*"The term "social business" will become more ubiquitous as organizations of all types and sizes start to*

*think of social technologies more strategically as business tools, not just marketing channels. And then it will eventually become a meaningless phrase as we come to realize that all business is, at its core, social."*

This is a complete about turn. Now executives are telling us that companies need to become more social. Of course there is a precedent for this, like telephone calls, then email access, then the company mobile phone. New technologies are always seen as damaging to the enterprise, but end up being adopted as essential.

McClure is arguing that social media is going to fundamentally change companies and how they operate. Forget about social media being just a tool for PR or marketing or community building - it is changing every part of the enterprise, root and branch.

If you don't believe me, take a look at your personal life. You probably have an online diary, address book and news feed with information on current affairs as well as what your friends are up to.

Let's just call it Facebook.

But whether it is Facebook or not, you have tools easily available that let you talk without cost to your family overseas, to find out which friend of your friends went to the same university as you, to find out which of your friends is around in New York when you are visiting.

This is taken for granted in your personal life. So your own life really is social and connected, yet most companies still languish with systems that cost millions and have never really worked. Imagine if you had the same level of knowledge about your colleagues at work, and your customers, as you have about your friends online.

Can you just imagine that? I mean really? We take it for granted now that we can communicate with friends and family globally yet once in the office it's a nightmare trying to get a conference call together with teams in three time zones.

Companies are just collections of people, with various skills, all attempting to pull in the same direction. Companies are social, yet we often use better tools to organize our social life than to organize how we work.

McClure from Thomson Reuters is absolutely correct, business is not "going social" because of social media tools; it already is social, we just need to learn how work more effectively with the tools around us.

## The cultural shock

But most executives have not spent their career working in social businesses, so this can be a difficult transition to make. When you hear an executive arguing that social media is just for the young, in a way they are right, but think about it like this.

The Netscape Navigator web browser launched in 1994 making it easy for anyone to access the World Wide Web – prior to that it really was the preserve of 'boffins' and geeks. Facebook launched a decade later in 2004 creating a new burst of energy as social networks consumed the Internet.

We are now twenty years on from easy web access and a decade on from the birth of Facebook. This means that the young graduates in your company right now, possibly already in junior management positions, do not remember a world where there was no Internet or mobile telephones. They have grown up always being connected to a personal phone and always having the ability to access any information at any time.

Now do you think that this is a trend you can really ignore? The big year for social media was really 2006[2]. This was when networks like Flickr and YouTube started growing and Facebook opened itself up to the general public – rather than just the students of a few Ivy-League colleges in the USA.

Even so, it was 2008 - or even 2009 - before social networks started to become ubiquitous. This was when they started appearing on adverts and TV shows would begin with a hashtag so that Twitter users knew how to engage with each other during the live show.

If a child were just entering their teens as this activity was taking place in 2006 to 2008 then they would already be 21 as I write. This means that there are not only young adults already in work with college degrees and no memory of life before the Internet, there are now people working in your company who quite literally cannot remember a time before social networking.

Feeling old now?

## So what can you do to catch up?

This book is generally focused on blogging and working with ghostwriters who can help executives to build their online presence, but it is hard to build any online presence for an executive that remains entirely ignorant of the social web.

When email was first introduced, it used to be common for executives to have their emails printed by a secretary who would deliver the reams of paper to their boss. The executive would scribble notes on the paper and expect the secretary to follow up by sending replies.

This sounds archaic today and we will feel the same within a couple of years if executives are not socially visible. Even if they have some support to help them blog regularly, they need to be aware of what is going on online.

But most executives argue that they have no time to be publishing details of their travel and eating plans online, and what is the point anyway. 'Who wants to know all this stuff?' is a common reaction.

I was once asked to talk to the managing partners of a big consulting firm in London. Their marketing team had convinced the partners that they should all be present on Twitter, but a glance at what they were publishing revealed messages like:

'I'm so tired, it's a long flight to Bangalore.'

'I hate the London Underground, I should have taken a taxi!'

'Had a great breakfast with a client today.'

It was no surprise that the partners in the firm were giving up on Twitter as a marketing tool. Nobody was following them for their latest update on which train or taxi they were using and they were not getting anything from providing these banal updates.

In fact, these messages reflect how Twitter looked back in the early days of 2007 and 2008. It was originally structured as a status update with the prompt asking 'what are you doing right now' and then a box allowing you to enter a 140-character update.

It is no surprise that the early tweets posted on Twitter do look quite banal as users initially considered a tweet to literally be a status update. My own first tweet just told the world that I was about to go to sleep.

The use of hashtags (#topichere) allowed people to start connecting together tweets on a single topic. For example if I am commenting on a World Cup football game then I would write my tweet and add the text #worldcup, allowing other users to just monitor anyone anywhere including that text in their tweets.

Twitter matured into more of an online conversation. It is still the single social network where the most engagement and conversation takes place, but you need to step back and think about how you are going to engage. Don't make the mistake the consulting firm did and just tell the senior managers to all get tweeting. Listen first.

## Get started

You can create a buzz about an idea or product very quickly and use the short 140-character messages to promote something far more substantial than these short messages suggest – with a little planning and thought.

As the consulting firm found out, you don't need to be endlessly publishing tweets – commenting on your day for example. Many executives ask why they would need to be tweeting what they had for breakfast and who might even be interested in this nonsense anyway?

You will find that the real value of Twitter is in listening to the conversations of others.

These are simple things you can try with a brand new corporate Twitter account:

1. Find and follow the key influencers in your industry. They might be the journalists who write about your business, the industry analysts, the consultants who recommend companies to clients, or even other executives in your industry. They are all on there – go and follow them. You can use a directory service like muckrack.com or manageflitter.com to help find interesting people.
2. Now add some search terms that are specific to your industry – so you are monitoring specific people and topics mentioned by anyone.
3. Now just watch and listen... all the messages on screen will either be from trusted people who are influencers in your industry or people talking about the subjects you are interested in.
4. Engage with those people – just talk to them. Comment on what they say and post a link to information online that might be relevant to the discussions you can already see taking place.

As you can see, these simple steps can make the value of Twitter obvious – what are people saying about your company or the products you sell right now? They are almost certainly talking about your brand – is anyone listening? More importantly, is anyone engaging in that debate?

# Customer Service and Social Media

If you still need convincing that social media is changing the way companies operate, then consider one part of every company that interacts with the public – the customer service team.

Customer service used to be a controlled activity. There would be a free phone number customers could call to comment or complain about a product. Later most companies added an email address or even a way to reach them via chat software, but in all these channels the company was choosing how the customer could get in touch.

Now this has been reversed. Customers are using social media tools, product review websites, forums and discussion boards and making comments or complaints online without ever directly addressing their comment to the brand *yet they still expect an answer*.

In fact if a brand like a cable TV provider or broadband ISP did not respond to online criticism on Facebook or Twitter then the customers would start behaving as if they have been ignored so the integration of social channels into customer service has become absolutely critical to brands in almost every industry today.

But more importantly, social customer service is transparent and can be amplified – so if there is a great example of customer service then it can be easily shared with friends and followers by a customer saying 'hey look at this great company and what they said to me'.

Likewise, the opposite is true as well when customer service is not as expected, customers can share a disappointing response and get it in front of thousands of their friends within seconds.

None of this applied when customers would telephone a call center and talk to an agent one on one. If they were not happy about the call then they might talk to the supervisor, but unless they made a recording of the call there would be no way of informing the world just how unhappy they are with the service from this brand.

So social media has changed the customer service function in almost every company in every industry you can think of. Those customer service agents are becoming the best marketing and sales tool your organization has, which is why the best place for any official executive communication is also inside the social web.

As McClure from Reuters said, companies themselves are changing the way they are structured. We have seen companies become collectives of expertise, more readily able to draw on partners with a more porous definition of exactly where the boundary of the organization is located, but now this concept of the global and social company is moving away from the IT sector and into the mainstream across all industries.

# Chapter 5: CEOs Must be Able to Talk to Customers

I t's worth taking a moment to think about the effect of some of these changes on how your executive team and the wider company interact with customers.

It's time to open our eyes. The customer service function is one of the most dynamic and exciting areas of business to be working in today. But it was not always like this. In fact, there are many people today who still consider that a contact center is a warehouse full of people reading a script halfway across the world.

Times have changed. This may come as a surprise to those who believe that the customer service function is still just a back-office department – a cost. It's fast becoming the most important part of every business in every industry. It's not stuck in the back-office; it is the eyes and ears of your business, your sales team, and your marketing team. It is your everything today.

Think back to the traditional view of how an organization is structured – the kind of hierarchical chart you might have studied in business school. Most of the business units are quite discrete units – separated from each other and reporting up to the executive management.

Think about that for a moment. That really is most companies today. The CEO sits at the top with an enormous span of control to the executive team one level down. Each of them represents a department and they all report upwards.

But this also means that people involved in sales or marketing or operations may have no daily contact with customers at all. They are too busy worrying about internal communications, budgets, strategies, and frequent flyer points...

But customer contact with brands has now exploded into a multidimensional array of channels. Many of them are transparent and can be shared to demonstrate an example of great service - or awful service. Even fairly 'regular' customers will already be familiar with half a dozen ways to get in touch with a brand.

Does that sound like an exaggeration? Think about voice calls, email, online chat, Twitter, Facebook, and online review sites like Tripadvisor. Half a dozen channels are now just normal. It's average. Everyone is using those channels, but you can add others such as WhatsApp, other social networks, blogs, and customer discussion forums... the list goes on and grows all the time.

Customer service is no longer a function that just focuses on dealing with customer problems. This is now where customers will get in touch before, during, and after a purchase. It's the place where the customer engages with the brand – it is now where you are building a relationship with the customer that you hope will be an enduring long-term one. Remember that word - relationship.

Some 'department' leaders can see this. Why do you think marketing directors across the world are aligning themselves with the customer service team? They don't want those grubby customer service directors to take over the marketing empire they have spent years developing in expensive wine bars.

If the customer service team are building relationships with potential – and existing customers – and engaging with them on a daily basis then that has a direct impact on every other business unit in the company. These are the true advocates of your brand, the people actually talking to customers every day and learning about their real needs.

This is not just a case of companies taking customer service more seriously as a department within their company; it is a fundamental reshaping of how any business operates today. In the long-term, this may completely change what we think of as a 'company' today, but what are the immediate consequences of this changing approach to corporate structure?

I believe that three conclusions can be drawn immediately from what is taking place in company boardrooms as they argue about customer service strategies today:

1.  A career in customer service is becoming a real career, not just a flexible job. Working in the contact center is no longer something you do while studying at college to do something else – getting that exposure to real customers can really lead you somewhere in the business. It could be operations, sales, marketing, or strategy. All of these teams will benefit from new team members who know what the customer is thinking.
2.  I believe that future executives will be severely disadvantaged if they have not done some time in a contact center. Companies will demand that their executives can relate directly to their customers. Moving from the contact center into sales or marketing then executive management will be far more common than crunching the numbers in finance

and getting picked for the top job because you understand tax law better than anyone else.

3. Customer service itself is getting better and is more focused on relationships. Every time I fly with British Airways I usually have a short Twitter exchange with them about the movies or other services available on the flight. Replying to me might be hard to measure in terms of marketing Return on Investment (ROI), but if I reach out with a comment to an airline and nobody ever answers me then I would certainly notice that they are ignoring me.

Customer service is moving into an era of engagement where customer loyalty is focused more on long-term relationships than loyalty cards and points. In fact, we will probably start redefining the terms we use – perhaps moving to "lifetime customer engagement" or "customer relationship management" – rather than just "customer service."

One thing is clear though; this is a dynamic area of business that is changing faster than any other function. Of course your next CEO is working in the contact center today.

Where else are you going to find the best leaders who can relate to what your customers really want?

And what else does this mean? CEOs are really going to understand how important it is to communicate well – it's not just an action to be taken by a hired agency. It may still be a challenge today, but it's going to get easier; I'm convinced of that.

# Chapter 6: What is the Best Online Channel to Promote Your Business?

The real question is how do your customers know about your company and the services or products you offer? Think about it for a moment. Let's forget about consumer products and strong brand images and just consider how a B2B organization can promote what it does to the world:

- **Advertising**. You can use online advertising such as Google Adwords to ensure that when people search for something related to what you are offering, your ad comes up in the search results. SEO can also be used to improve organic search results. Of course, you could also buy posters by the side of a road, but that's another story.
- **Editorial**. If a business or trade publication documents what you do, using your firm as a case study then that is much more powerful than an advert, but it requires a process of public relations – getting to know the right journalists.
- **Analysts**. Most industries have a community of analysts studying the companies on their beat and writing detailed reports about financial performance and plans for the future. Many analysts publish comparisons showing which companies are the strongest in their area – for instance the Magic

Quadrant published by Gartner. Clearly it is important to keep these people updated.

- **Consultants**. When a business needs a partner they will often go to a consulting firm and ask them to study the problem and select a partner. If the consulting firms don't know you, then it is unlikely you will ever be selected as a part of the solution for their clients.
- **Existing customers**. The executives running your existing customer base meet their peers and have a network within their own industry so it's important to ensure that they know what you are up to, beyond just the day-to-day delivery.
- **Employees**. Your employees are almost certainly connected to peers outside the company and as people move around the industry they are potentially your next clients. It's worth asking the question: would you buy from your own company?
- **Networking**. Trade shows, conferences, all the events where buyers and sellers gather to explore what is taking place in the industry.
- **Partnerships**. Trade bodies or think tanks are worth exploring as a way of thinking about the future and creating ideas without just offering a hard sell on your current products.

That's a long list and I am not going to suggest that blogging is a silver bullet that can address every concern, but used well, it is a strategy that can address different audiences. This can work especially well if you delineate your audience around the various social networks, broadly addressing a different audience depending on the network you are using.

For example, one of my existing clients uses the following methodology:

- **Determine the topics:** the sales team generally define the topics that should be discussed on the blog because they are the ones who will use this content to generate meetings and interest in the company. The content needs to reflect what they want to say to potential clients, or at least reflect that the company is competent and has great insights into the industry you operate within.
- **Create blogs**: it is important to have something to talk about, rather than just inanely tweeting about the news of the day. The regular publication of blogs gives a central core to their communication activity and can be used to start conversations with people they want to interact with online – in any network and for any kind of influencer.
- **Ask managers to post on LinkedIn**: every member of the management team will ensure that a blog post published in their name is also featured on their own LinkedIn profile and many of them will just publish all of the blogs being published by the company on their LinkedIn Pulse. This ensures that their professional network is exposed to the content being created.
- **Tweet for analysts and influencers**: Twitter is full of journalists, analysts, and consultants all seeking information on the companies they are interested in so it's important to make sure they see you have an opinion on the industry.
- **Facebook for the team**: a Facebook 'fan' page can be a useful way to have a lighter more fun engagement with current and past employees. It's like a virtual alumni group allowing photos and ideas to be shared.

The important thing to notice about this strategy is that there is no formal PR involved and no advertising at all. Why? Because all of the people a B2B needs to reach can usually be accessed through these other channels.

Traditional PR is anachronistic in the modern world of journalism. Think about the way B2B PR used to work. A company would engage an agency to act as their link to the world of journalism. It was dark and mysterious and connections were protected because the real stardust a good agency could offer was a hotline to the important writers.

The agency would prepare press releases every time the company had something to say about a new client, or their latest financial results, or a new product, and these would be dispatched to individual journalists or sent to PR networks that would send the releases on to journalists who had expressed an interest in that topic.

I still get releases like this. I got one this morning for a new app developed by a software company in India. Apparently women can add this app to their smart phone and when they feel in danger of being raped, it can be used to trigger an alert to friends and family. It's not a subject to be mocked and I know that India has an increasing problem with rape, but the app sounds more like a solution looking for a problem. If a family member of mine was in similar danger I'd rather she calls the cops than starts messing around with an app that calls her friends.

I delete 99 percent of the press releases that arrive in my inbox, as most are impersonal and not really of interest. It also offends me that a decade into the world of social media, allowing short, direct, personal messages, I still have to tolerate this deluge from PR agencies who operate on a scattergun principle – if you send the message to enough journalists and bloggers then at least some of them will pay attention.

Now consider how a journalist – or blogger – really works. They usually have a beat they are focused on so if you have a story that is on their beat then they are probably going to be interested. However, this interest will be diminished if the news has come from an anonymous PR press release that just hits the slush pile with other releases. If the head of sales at your company tweets a writer directly and says 'hey, would you like to chat over lunch about our just published numbers?' then that's a very different story.

Alternatively, the writer might be kicking their heels. It's a slow day at the office and they are not sure what to write about. Take a look at Twitter in the morning and you will often see journalists saying something like "I'm thinking about [add subject here] today, anyone got any ideas?"

If it's something your company is involved in and the writer gets a tweet back from your CEO saying "let's talk, we are doing that in 99 countries" then you can expect a call. The journalist wants to write about you. Contact the right people and they are happy to talk, just like advertising is no longer annoying when it is so personalized that it is helpful.

The mysterious "dark art" of managing journalists and bloggers has vanished. If I am interested in technology writers in Britain, then I can ask Google for "UK technology journalists twitter list" and various lists of influential writers are returned immediately.

So let's consider the example of the client and what they achieve from the various activities they undertake:

# The Blog

The blog is your own corporate voice, like a magazine you can use to publish anything you want. Of course some companies believe this means that it should be just the same announcements that used to be sent as press releases, but more enlightened leaders realize that they can use a blog to voice their opinion and to demonstrate their knowledge and competence.

When all the other promotional activities are being undertaken to try engaging with influencers in your industry, being able to demonstrate that you also have a voice and might even agree with an influencer is a valuable asset. It prevents the impression that you have just hired a marketing professional to sit there tweeting "look at me, look at me!"

Corporate blogs usually don't achieve a large audience, but just having it there gives you a central core on which to base your other online promotional activities.

It's worth mentioning that blogs are not as interactive as they used to be. Some blogs never receive a single comment today, even if they get a good amount of readers. This is because much of the discussion around blogs now takes place on other social channels. Instead of commenting directly on a blog, many readers will now share it on Facebook or Twitter with a comment there such as 'have you read this nonsense?'

# LinkedIn

This is traditionally the "business" network where people maintain their business connections. It has grown in stature over the past few years and is now a very useful way to keep in touch with the people in your business network – making it easy to keep track of people when they change job or take on a new role in the same company.

LinkedIn has a number of discussion groups where people involved in the same industry can get together to discuss topics. This has typically been where companies have tried to promote their wares on the network, but usually this is a failure.

Who wants to go and join the discussion group "XYZ call centers, let's talk call centers here" when you know it's a group managed by XYZ with the purpose of selling their services?

A better strategy is just to get your own team to leverage their network. Each of your managers is probably connected to a few hundred people on LinkedIn, just get them publishing your blog content on their own newsfeed and it will be noticed by the people connected to the management team – simple.

The blog platform "Pulse" built into LinkedIn is a powerful way to reuse any content you are publishing on the corporate blog too.

If you are publishing blogs in the name of the CEO then ask him or her to post it on their personal LinkedIn blog too. The people in their personal business network will see it. Corporate blogs often get more traction inside LinkedIn than just publishing and hoping the right audience will find it. With LinkedIn the executive will have built up their audience by connecting to people over a number of years, so it should be in front of the right readers very quickly.

# Twitter

This is the big online conversation. Millions of tweets everyday on every topic in every country mean that someone, somewhere is talking about your products, your company, or your industry.

You can engage with those people who are already talking about something relevant or you can create a "hit list" of key influencers. Follow them, watch what they say and interject when they are talking about something related to what your business does. Or just retweet them if what they are saying sounds profound – or just interesting.

Watching the key influencers in your industry and then engaging them on Twitter is enormously valuable, especially for a B2B organization. You can watch what the key journalists, analysts, and consultants in your industry are up to and then interact with them as you choose.

Having some good blog content to back you up helps avoid the impression that you are a child raising your hand in front of a teacher too – show that you also have a view on this business. You also have expertise and an opinion.

# Facebook

Facebook is a great tool for building and managing a community. It has become less powerful than it used to be because group managers posting content into a page now realize that not every group member will see the content – Facebook wants extra cash for that to happen – but it remains a good way to create a group and to then allow them to interact informally.

For this reason, it's a great way for existing employees to post pictures of activities in their area – a charity event for example – and as people leave the company they will usually stay in the group, allowing access to this alumni group too.

# Advertising

If an executive in a B2B organization asked their team about a strategy for advertising and editorial engagement with journalists today then the conversation cannot be undertaken within the framework of 'column inches' and 'Advertising Value Equivalency' (AVE – basically meaning if you can get a mention for free in the editorial then how much would that have cost as an advert). The world has changed.

Just before the London Olympic games in 2012, the British government launched their GREAT campaign. This is a global information campaign aimed at promoting tourism and trade with the UK and though I believe the broad campaign has a great deal of merit, I remember a specific example of promotional activity in 2012 that shocked me.

The launch party in Brazil was at the Sugar Loaf Mountain in Rio de Janeiro, a beautiful location where the government had recreated a London pub, scattered some James Bond memorabilia around, and invited Prince Harry to speak as the guest of honor. In terms of getting the UK noticed, whatever they spent on this party did the trick because every journalist and blogger in Brazil wanted to be there – especially the girls who just wanted to meet Harry.

But on the day of the event, as I walked around Rio, I noticed that most of the bus stops in the city had the UK GREAT branding printed all over them. There were big photographs of British towns plastered all over these bus stops in downtown Rio.

When I talked to the executives responsible for the campaign launch they talked enthusiastically about the AVE created by the party, but when I asked who had approved the idea of branding every bus stop in Rio, I was greeted with an embarrassed silence. I never got a satisfactory answer and I assume it was just one of those things where an advertising budget was approved and needed to be spent on something, even though they were already doing other activities that were smarter and more likely to be noticed.

After all, bus stop advertising might work for a film company trying to announce the release of a new movie, but how many people were catching the bus to Rio that week and pulled out their smart phone to book a trip to Edinburgh because they saw a photo at the bus stop? I haven't checked the figures, but my guess is precisely zero.

Editorial and advertising are being blurred in some journals. There has always been infomercial and advertorial in newspapers and magazines, the adverts written as if they are a part of the paper, but with a discreet 'ADVERTISEMENT' message, but this has developed further.

The news site Buzzfeed is a great example of the new world order. Though it often appears to just be a site full of lists, such as '27 great things about living in New York' or '32 reasons you can only be Canadian' they have found that this list format is popular online – people love to share these lists. And real news can also be reported this way.

Buzzfeed is one of the fastest growing news organizations in the world today, hiring real journalists with expert knowledge, but then getting them to present news in a way that will encourage people to share it. Examples would include government budget analysis '10 ways the budget affects you' or foreign policy '25 facts you need to know about Ukraine'.

Buzzfeed has built a reputation for this type of news and instead of carrying banner adverts all over the site they just mix sponsor-promoted content with the 'real' content. So it could be Nike offering a list of training and performance tips or Coca Cola offering tips on hydration in hot weather.

This kind of advertising activity is less relevant to the B2B community, but the way in which news is created and consumed affects us all. The way companies of all sizes and types inform potential customers about their products has changed beyond recognition and your clients will need to understand this – if they are still thinking of advertising as just a poster-sized image of George Clooney standing next to your product.

# Chapter 7: How Could I Start Tomorrow?

You can start on a blogging and social media strategy tomorrow. You could even do it today. There is no cost for most of the tools you are going to use, however it is worth sitting back and thinking about what you want to achieve and how you are going to do it before just reaching for your iPhone and installing the Twitter app.

Despite it not costing a penny to load up Twitter on your iPhone there is going to be some cost associated with doing this well. Before loading those apps, consider the following areas:

- **Strategy**. What is it that you plan to achieve from blogging and becoming a socially active executive? Every company wants to achieve more sales, but what is the funnel of activity in your industry that leads a manager to buy from your company and can your engagement with traditional influencers help you to get in front of more potential buyers?

- **Measurements**. Every finance director wants to understand the Return on Investment (ROI) before undertaking a new initiative. In many cases this can be hard to define in dollar terms with a communication initiative, but it may be possible to define the cost of **not** undertaking the project in that same way that consumer brands can no longer afford to ignore messages about their products on social media. Sometimes you need to think of the opportunity cost.

- **Guidelines**. When you know what you want to achieve and have some idea of how any costs will be budgeted, the actual activities need to be planned. This requires setting out roles, responsibilities, and actions. Who will be writing content? Who will be checking and approving it? Who will be publishing content? Who will be promoting blogs? There is a need to define how the program will work even if most of the activities are to be taken on by existing members of your team.

- **Training**. Your team needs to be involved. It's unlikely that you can achieve much success flying solo as the super-connected CEO. In fact, if you are the only one projecting that image in your company, then it will not look very connected. But some in your team are going to be worried about this initiative. Some are not going to believe in it. Some are still going to think that all this blogging business is just about publishing selfies. You need a training program that tells them why it's important and how they can get involved.

- **Editorial content or blogs**. Once you know approximately what you want to do and who will be involved, you will need to start creating some content. This could be blog posts, it could be blog posts combined with some social activity, or it could just be social messages. In my opinion, it's always useful for a business leader to have a bedrock of opinion on a blog in addition to just posting messages on Facebook or Twitter, but however you do it will probably need support from a writer or team member who can write quickly and authoritatively.

# The critical path

Let's take a typical B2B campaign as an example and consider what you need to get in place and who needs to do what to make it work. I'm assuming that you want to start publishing a corporate blog twice a week in the name of your CEO and then to promote that blog and to use the blog in a way that can help you reach out to key influencers in your industry.

Every engagement is different, but this is a typical requirement: create good content, promote it, and then leverage on the content to create connections and engagement with people who matter. So, based on this scenario and the questions listed earlier, what do you need to do to get started tomorrow?

# Before you start

Let's skip past all the strategic decision-making. You have decided that you want to do this. The boss needs to be blogging and engaging with the key influencers in your industry. You figured out that this is important and you want to start, but what needs to be planned before you start?

# Who will be working on this?

You are not going to start creating all this content alone. In fact, you might not be creating any of the content at all or any of the social activity, but someone will need to do that. You need to find a blogger or journalist or a marketing or PR agency that can help. If you are the CEO and this content is going to be published in your name, then you need to be comfortable with whoever is going to be writing on your behalf.

This is where I have found my own personal approach to helping tech CEOs valuable when compared to the more general help an agency can offer. Of course, there are also some great agencies out there that offer this kind of service. The point is that whoever you hire to create words in your name needs to understand your business and must be able to write in your voice.

## What will these people do?

Are you hiring a writer alone or do you expect your content producer to also upload the content to a blog, find nice images to illustrate the point, add keywords, and generally make sure that everything is actually published? And if you have a social strategy connected to the blog, to promote the blog and reach out to influencers then is it going to be the same person who is creating the content or will you separate these roles allowing one team to create the content and another to promote it?

## Who will contribute?

If your blog posts are all going to be written by a single author then this is less of a concern, if that author can schedule a quick call or email every couple of weeks then the ghostwriter can stay on top of their thoughts.

But if you want to have a pool of contributors, that requires a bit more organization. Everyone included in the contributor pool needs to know that they have been included and what area of the business they are expected to comment on as well as how often they need to comment.

It should also be agreed who will chase them when they inevitably forget to send their ideas to the writing team – should the ghostwriter be chasing them for a comment or will the main communications team ensure there is a flow of ideas to the ghostwriter?

## Who do we want to reach?

Your team must have a plan of action when it comes to the influencer community. It's no good to just say that you want to be noticed by the New York Times. Who are the real influencers in your business area?

Perhaps you want the big industry analyst firms like Gartner, Ovum, Frost & Sullivan, Forrester, and IDC to notice your activity, but there may also be niche analysts focused on your specific activity. And though it's great to be noticed by the biggest journalists in the world, a more realistic target for everyday activity might be the trade journalists covering your business area each day of the week.

Influencers will come and go and change over time, but you need to ensure that right from the start there is at least some kind of hit list to start following as these are the people who will be monitored.

In addition to being noticed by the influencers in your business area, if you work with your sales team to get input into blog topics then the blog can support them as they knock on doors and chase prospects. For example, if your sales team is working hard to win business from a retailer then why not blog about some of the issues those prospects are facing – then the sales team can use that content in their initial conversations. Blogs can open doors too.

## Ongoing responsibilities

In almost all the projects I have worked on, almost all of the activities mentioned are outsourced to the writing team – the writing, uploading, and promotion on social media.

This is because most marketing or communications teams are busy and under pressure and if a company or individual comes along and offers a service that relieves them of some pressure then that service is agreed on immediately.

So in the hypothetical example of a contract where two new blogs are going to be created each week, the ongoing responsibilities and activities might be something like this:

1. The CEO needs to update the writing team with his or her latest ideas – topics to be blogged. This doesn't need to be on a daily or weekly basis, but once or twice a month getting direct contact from the CEO can ensure that the content stays focused on what is relevant to the business;
2. At the start of the week, the writing team should create the draft content and send it to the internal communications team to be checked;
3. The communications team should have the authority to check and approve the content. If the approvals procedure requires multiple managers to check the content or even the CEO in person then it is probably

going to be too slow. Remember that the blog content is likely to be short (100-200 word) comments on industry news or strategies, instead of press releases;

4. The writing team should publish the approved content on the blog with relevant keywords and some additional media such as relevant photos or video that support the content – all this content can be legally added with no cost just be searching for Creative Commons (cc) content;

5. The writing team can promote the specific blog by tweeting about it, and adding it to any other specific company networks such as Facebook or LinkedIn;

6. On an ongoing basis, the writing team will monitor the 'hit list' of interesting influencers, retweeting any valuable comments and engaging with a comment where appropriate.

The above model places a great deal of responsibility with the writer, or the writing team. They are expected to communicate with the boss to get ideas, articulate those ideas as pithy blogs, ensure the client approves the content, upload it, promote it, and monitor the Internet to see if anyone is saying anything worth interacting with.

However, in most cases, this will be the only feasible way to make a blogging program work – because every communications professional in the team is already busy. If the new blogging program the CEO wants to launch expects the internal team to start monitoring and engaging with key influencers, then either the internal team needs to get bigger or it just won't happen once the program gets going.

# Fake engagement

Of course, CEOs, politicians, and other important leaders have their speeches written for them. And since the press started publishing articles by business leaders, they have employed journalists to draft words that would be published in their name.

So how can ghost blogging be fake?

There is nothing wrong in supporting a CEO, in helping them to articulate their ideas into blogs and then publishing them in the name of the CEO.

But for a social media program to work and avoid the accusation of just being marketing spin, it is important to involve the real person in responding to comments and questions.

For example, as I mentioned earlier, the writing team may use the Twitter account of the CEO to promote the published blogs and to watch over the influencer hit list – reaching out and saying hello when an influencer mentions an area that would be of interest to the business.

I have a golden rule with all my clients for whom I do this kind of work. I will never engage in a conversation with anyone online using a named social media account and pretending to be that person. Everyone has a right to believe that if they are chatting to someone on a tool like Twitter, then it is the real person answering their questions.

I don't know if this applies to every business leader online. When I see the amount of content Sir Richard Branson manages to publish – blogs, video, and photos – each day I can see that he obviously has the Virgin communications team supporting him, but I do wonder if the real Sir Richard would reply if I messaged him? I hope so, and I have seen him blogging about how he really does interact with his readers[1].

I was once talking about the James Bond movie 'The Spy Who Loved Me' with a friend, Peter Ryan, on Twitter. We were talking about the Lotus car that can travel underwater. I asked him if he knew where the scene was filmed where Roger Moore drives the car out of the sea onto a beach full of tourists. We both thought it was Malta, but then Sir Roger Moore tweeted the correct answer, "Sardinia."[2]

Peter and I were astounded, but when I recounted the story to someone else, he just dismissed it and said it was a PR or film company hack using the Roger Moore account.

I hope not. Tools like Twitter are very personal. If you are representing a CEO and ensuring that their account remains active with tweets on the latest news and rumors in their industry, that support has to stop when people send messages and expect the real person to respond.

Even if your writing team is using the Twitter account of the CEO to promote blogs and monitor the hit list, if anyone sends a message then your team needs to alert the named individual and get them to respond personally. So in this example, the writing team would need to be able to send a text or email directly to the CEO asking him or her to check their Twitter account.

The executive embarking on a social media program cannot be entirely ignorant of how these tools work. They need Twitter installed on their iPad or phone even if they don't look at it on a day-to-day basis. But when that journalist from the New York Times sends a tweet asking a question about what the company thinks on a specific topic there is no way you want a marketing or writing team member to be replying to that message – public or privately.

Always involve the management team in your online content activities. If they are putting their name to blogs and tweets then they must be available to answer questions online even if they have a support team helping to generate the original content.

Think of it like ghostwriting a speech. You can prepare the words and feed the lines to your CEO, but when the Q&A begins, there is no prepared script; they need to know their own business.

# Chapter 8: Exploring Value and Measuring Success

After reading this far and seeing not only how social networks and blogs have changed in the past few years, but also how much our model of communication itself has changed, you might be asking 'how do I measure if any of this actually works?'

Taking a social approach to your business has a number of advantages, but it is worth considering exactly what you are trying to achieve by exploring social media.

Just because everyone in the business press is now discussing this topic, does not mean that creating a Facebook page and blog for your company will lead to automatic success.

Think back and consider all of the reasons why you might be exploring social media and blogging;

- **Marketing and advertising**. This is the most likely area for most people reading this book. You want to explore how to promote your company, create visibility and most importantly earn revenue from new clients who might not have heard of your company before;
- **Improving your own service**. It could be that the service you offer can be dramatically improved by engaging more socially;

- **Interaction and engagement.** Clients are expecting a lot more social interaction with companies these days and many companies have started building communities of clients and interested parties – the engagement can be online or offline, but is often facilitated using online tools.
- **Creating Loyalty.** Engagement with customers and the vast amounts of data companies can now draw on and analyze using 'Big Data' tools means that loyalty is moving towards discounts and deals specifically designed for each individual customer. It's time to bin the loyalty cards.
- **Internal communications.** Engaging more openly and more socially can improve the way your own company communicates internally – for example by getting the management to team to blog and allowing staff (and alumni) at all levels to make comments.

There could be many reasons why you want to engage more socially, but let's assume that the most important reasons for you are:

- Improving your revenue – getting more sales;
- Improving your visibility – finding new customers who were not aware of you;
- Improving your outreach – being able to reach into markets that previously seemed impossible to tap into.

Fortunately, it is possible for you to achieve this with a little planning, some of which I have covered earlier in this book. Social media allows access across borders and can help you to find new clients, but it does need a slightly different approach to any sales drive you may have arranged in the past.

One important point to remember is that many markets have globalised very rapidly in the past few years. Companies are prepared to look further for products and services, but that also means that there is global competition.

Always try to remember: how does a company executive who needs to buy a service find a potential partner? They will almost always start by searching the Internet to see who is selling in that area, regardless of where they are located.

Doing business locally is still good, but now it is easy to find the best partner, regardless of where they are based.

There are three very important factors that you need to take into consideration when thinking of how to communicate in the social environment:

## 1. Transparency

The assumption on most social networks is that any conversation between the company representative and the customer (or potential customer) is open and visible to all, whether as Twitter messages or a Facebook wall discussion.

Calls to a contact center are all recorded, but other customers would not listen in to calls, so there is a very different open discourse taking place in this new environment – where one customer might even have the answer sought by another and be happy to share it.

This difference is crucial. Sometimes you will just be facilitating a discussion between your own customers or prospects – not directly selling to them. Much of this discussion will take place before or during a sale – unlike the old days, when this customer interaction happened almost entirely post-sale.

With value being placed on the transparency of communication, it is important to be honest about what you can do and how. It's not possible to pitch to a prospect in a social environment when you know all of their online friends can also see your pitch – the traditional sales pitch does not work in this environment.

## 2. Amplification

Whether the experience is good or bad, it is very easy for customers to amplify something they see online by sharing it with their online friends – which goes back to my earlier point about changing the way you interact with potential or existing customers online.

This idea of amplification works both ways and can be very positive for you – or negative.

Imagine you are dealing with an existing customer online, who is making a complaint about your service within a social network. If you can address the complaint online using the same network, openly answering their comments and helping to resolve the issue, then it is just as likely the customer will broadcast their satisfaction to all of their online friends.

Being able to turn around a complaint like this and to create a customer who sings your praises is referred to as the creation of brand advocates. When everyone today can be a publisher, every customer can help to promote your products.

However, if you try to sell to someone you don't know in a way that is seen as intrusive, the potential customer might send a message to all his or her contacts saying something like "don't ever deal with this joker – look at the way he is trying to sell to me."

This is a very open and transparent environment and you should always assume that communications are be seen by everyone – unless they are specifically kept private.

Amplification is a powerful concept and should be combined with the transparent approach to create scenarios where many customers and prospects are happy to show others a positive experience with your own organization.

# 3. Showcasing expertise

For most companies that are exploring any social outreach, a blog will need to be at the heart of what you do online.

You can use Twitter to talk to potential customers or influencers or create discussion groups on LinkedIn, but these other discussions are always going to be easier to start if you have a place where you are publishing your own thoughts and opinions.

Publishing in this way demonstrates your competence. It shows any potential customer that you have ideas and can talk about your business area in a way that shows insight and a willingness to innovate.

Imagine handing out your business cards to prospects in future and on the flip side of your card there is an invitation to talk about the issues in your industry on your blog. Isn't it likely that this will create a discussion in the meeting?

## Measuring Success

In this book I am focused mainly on the process of blogging and the use of social media to promote a B2B corporate blog so when talking about the measurement of success – or Return on Investment (ROI) – it is with this in mind that I am most focused.

A B2C campaign to promote a new chocolate bar might measure the success of the campaign by the levels of interaction, how many people shared a video or liked the campaign on Facebook. In the B2B environment, all these measurements are meaningless.

This presents a dilemma for the communications and marketing team. If all the traditional metrics used to measure the success of social media programs are useless, then how can we justify spending money on a campaign ourselves?

In the B2B environment there is still pressure to do it anyway, but not to the same extent as a company that is directly selling to consumers and simply must respond to any online discussion about their products.

Let's use the typical scenario that I have described earlier: a CEO blogging twice a week about his or her industry with social support to promote the blog. Managers in the team are sharing blog links on LinkedIn and there is support on Twitter to ensure the blogs are promoted and a hit list of influencers is engaged.

First, it is easier to define what we are not particularly interested in measuring:

- **Followers on Twitter.** Your CEO needs quality followers, rather than quantity. It is far better to have 20 or 30 high quality followers that are from the analyst and journalist community than 1,000 business school students.
- **Retweets on Twitter.** It's nice to see that people like what you said and are happy to share it with their own followers, but as with the follower count, unless it is an influencer you want to interact with then retweets are of very little benefit.
- **Klout score,** Klout schmout. There are many similar tools out there such as Kred and Peerindex (pi), but why would your CEO be worried about a measure of his or her influence on social networks? Just worry about being influential in your actual industry.
- **Blog readers.** Your blog may have relatively few readers for a number of reasons, but primarily because

people do not have a lot of time to seek out content that does not find them. If you can republish on LinkedIn Pulse and get a trade journal or blog to carry the blogs of your CEO – in addition to having them on your own corporate website – then you may develop a reasonable audience, but don't sweat about reader numbers. The blog is mainly there to help engage with the hit list of key influencers or prospects; you are not trying to start your own version of Forbes magazine.

- **Blog comments.** Blogs were around before the social networks and back then the comments on blogs would be as interesting and useful as the blog posts. Entire conversations and discussions could play out in the comments on many blogs. Now the comments section of most blogs is desolate, with virtual tumbleweed blowing around. This is because most discussion has moved to the social networks – if someone sees an interesting blog they will share it on Facebook, LinkedIn, or Twitter and engage in discussion with people there inside the social network.

- **Advertising Value Equivalency (AVE).** This may only apply if you are involving a PR agency in the social media program and it forms part of a wider communication plan. It is basically what agencies use to estimate how much some editorial exposure is worth – to get the same visibility by advertising would cost $x amount. It's always been a contentious measure and doesn't apply at all to an executive blogging program, even if the blogs do result in media coverage.

These are all typical metrics that social media managers or communications managers with a social responsibility would be interested in tracking.

Forget about them.

And while you are forgetting all these social measurements, you can tell the marketing director to stop worrying about all these other measures that are frequently cited as essential for anyone using social media:

- **Reach and audience growth rate.** It's nice to see your social audience growing, but not essential for this kind of blogger. You need to be reaching the right people, not more of the wrong people.
- **Visitor frequency rate**. Why waste time measuring how many times people return to your website or blog?
- **Conversions.** In our scenario we are not usually trying to sell directly so measures like conversion rates are pointless.
- **Activity savings.** Often the saving from performing a task online will be used to justify the project, if you can divert the action from a more expensive channel to social media then the company saves money, but in our scenario this is another measure you can forget about.

None of this is applicable to what is being proposed in this book. You are not a brand trying to grow awareness of a product using social media – and it is highly unlikely that you will make sales directly using these tools – though prospects can be warmed and doors opened. Stop thinking that you need to measure success in terms of Twitter followers.

In fact, I suspect that the growth in fake Twitter followers has been boosted by the need for so many social media managers to hit a specific target so they can achieve their end of year bonus.

Who is fooling whom with all this fake activity?

## What should be measured?

The critical measurements in our scenario are all linked to real business activity, but are generally linked to increasing engagement with the influencer community. It is possible that you may interact directly with a prospective customer online, but more likely – in a B2B firm - that your constant monitoring of a key hit list will yield good interactions that would not have been otherwise achieved – or would have been less effective.

The broad benefits our CEO might expect to achieve from the blogging and social media promotion program are:

- **Networking improvements.** There are probably key influencers that the CEO plans to have lunch with two or three times a year. Now that discussion can be continued between lunches and probably on a more friendly basis than possible when only meeting a few times a year.
- **Press coverage**. If the key journalists in the sector can easily reach this CEO before any other because he or she is socially available then they will probably be the first called on for industry comment and analysis.
- **Better analyst relationships**. The better the analyst community knows you, your company, and your views on where the industry is going, the more accurate their coverage and analysis of your business.
- **Prospect introductions**. If your sales team has managed to open doors to prospective customers by using blog content to ease their way into a

conversation then this is clearly a benefit that can result in new revenue if the deal is closed.

These benefits and outcomes are quite general and vague, because what is being suggested is that the real advantage comes from improved engagement with key industry influencers. The executive team, along with the communications team in your business, need to think of this as a new way of networking – focusing on engagement.

This engagement can take many forms, but some more specific ideas about what can be expected are:

- The leading industry analyst in your field is coming to visit your town. You tweet a welcome and suggest hanging out for a coffee, an offer that is accepted and you now have a much closer personal bond with a leading influencer in your field;
- A leading technology writer tweets that he would really like to talk to someone from a company that is involved in your area. You tweet a response and end up featured the following day in a major story as an expert industry commentator;
- The editor of a trade journal that is of interest to your business mentions that they would love some contributions from experts in your field. You ask if they would be interested in publishing some of your recent blogs and they agree to use the content in their journal;
- A leading consultant publishes a report giving their view on the future of your industry. You can tweet the author of the report directly and openly debate the analysis whether you agree or disagree – either way it shows the consulting firm that you are switched on and watching their output;

- A blogger publishes a story that trashes the reputation of your company. Before setting the lawyers on them you tweet the blogger – ensuring everyone online can see you are ready to openly engage – and suggest they come to your office to talk about their issues in person.

Clearly, many of these engagements can be defined as networking or improving an existing network, but this is quite scientific networking.

The CEO should be building a reputation online as a thought leader by publishing their opinion and ideas in addition to watching what the opinion formers and influencers in their industry are saying – and then being ready to engage.

So instead of measuring any metrics that are specific to social media or networks directly, think more about the business network of your CEO. Is the CEO lunching and conversing more often with the influencers in your industry because of the blog and social media program? If so, then that is the measure of your success.

# Chapter 9: What Makes a Content Strategy Fail?

In the last chapter I discussed how to measure success, however there are many steps along the path to achieving that first lunch with a critical influencer because they liked one of your tweets.

Along that path there are many factors that will lead your blogging program to either fail entirely or stagnate. You will be publishing information, but may see no results from all the effort of the team.

In the corporate blogging programs I have managed, I have seen the same distinct problems crop up time and again. In some cases they have been fatal and caused the closure of the entire social project, but usually the project can be turned around if the desire is there to save it.

I would summarize the key issues that can derail your blogging program as:

- **Scope creep.** There is some initial success and the client asks the support team to add another Twitter account, or add an extra blog a week, or add an emergency blog because something important happened. You keep adding requirements, but never add the support to make it work properly.
- **Executives too busy to be involved**. The support team needs guidance. They need the CEO or the executive team to be indicating the topics they want

blogged. They need the CEO to dial in for those status meetings so everyone is on the same page.

- **Hubris – or "Kevin Costner syndrome."** An assumption that if a blog is published then an audience will automatically come and find it – then disappointment when the CEO realizes that this is harder than expected. Try telling a CEO with an ego the size of Jupiter than only his mother retweeted his last witty comment on Twitter.
- **Bureaucracy**. The communications team wants to approve every word broadcast in the name of the company and are therefore tied up in layers of bureaucratic approval every time the support team wants to send out any public message.
- **Technophobia**. The CEO wants to be seen online as a blogger and tweeter, but doesn't bother installing any social media tools on his or her phone. The CEO takes no real interest in using the tools and assumes that the team can manage it all.
- **Inadequate commitment**. The communications team know they have to do something, but don't have much time of budget to make it happen, so they agree to publish one blog a month, without any promotion or engagement.

Let's explore each of these key issues in turn.

# Scope creep

This relates mainly to the relationship between the client and the supporting writer or content production company. There are various ways a content production team can be paid with the three most common being:

- Paid by unit of time, paying a writer by the day as an example
- Paid per unit of output, paying a writer for each article that is produced
- Paid a fixed retainer for an approximate amount of output, usually a per month fee with an expected amount of work agreed between the parties

I've been paid in all these various ways over the years, but the most common is the third option. Sit down with the client and agree on an expected amount of work and then agree on a fixed fee for that work.

That is also the best option for the client, because they can budget for the entire year, knowing exactly how much you will charge and the supplier gets the certainty of a regular monthly fee for an agreed amount of work.

But this fixed arrangement can cause a problem if the blog becomes popular and the client wants to publish more. Let's assume you contracted to blog twice a week and suddenly the client is asking for three or four blog entries in a week.

That's OK, if it is a particularly busy week. Nobody minds helping a client out if they have all their regular blogs, plus some comments on a big news story.

But when that happens the next week and then when someone from marketing suggests that you not only manage the Twitter account of the CEO, but also the CMO too, what can you do?

Fixed fee contracts can be renegotiated, but it is often difficult to do so because the manager controlling that budget will have told his boss how much the social media program is going to cost at the start of the year. Until the next financial year, that number can't change.

In most cases, the writing team involved just needs to accept the additional work - or lose the contract. But if this does happen, then it is because the program is working and it is important to agree on a review to the contract price at the time of the next budget review.

As anyone in business knows though, once a situation is normalized, that becomes the price for the job. If the scope expands in the middle of the year so you spend six months doing a lot more for the same price then by the time of the budget review that will now be the accepted price for that level of work. A difficult situation and one to be wary of.

## Executives too busy to be involved

The support team needs the executives who are named on the blog to be interested in what is getting published in their name. This may sound obvious, but the ideal scenario is when the CEO wants to be blogging, but just doesn't have the time or writing ability.

If they can see that having a writing team really helps them to reach more people and all they need to do is regularly feed the team some ideas then it can work well. But if the CEO loses interest and never gets back in touch after the initial project conversations, then what can the writing team do?

They will have a contract in place and a requirement to keep creating content. But with very little guidance, all they can do is keep on commenting on the same areas as before.

Of course, it may be that the writer knows the market very well and can continue to make intelligent comment based on their knowledge of the industry. The only issue is that this kind of current affairs commentary may not be where the company wants to be focusing attention.

A typical example of this happening is when status calls are endlessly postponed, never happen, or you just never get any reply at all from the CEO – even though they were initially excited.

This happens because busy people assume they can delegate the task of writing content and it should just continuously flow at an agreed rate, without any further input from them.

## Hubris, or "Kevin Costner syndrome"

I have seen CEOs publishing books that proclaim how well they know their industry, yet the books are little more than vanity projects.

I once met a CEO who spent around $100,000 licensing the images that were going to be printed in the book. I made the mistake of asking how on earth he was going to earn that cash back, but his reply was simple: "It's going to sell a lot of copies!"

This kind of hubris can often derail a blogging program if the expectations are not set and managed correctly early on. A CEO might see the millions of followers a business leader like Sir Richard Branson has and assume that once he or she starts blogging away the masses will flock to worship at their feet.

It's unlikely to happen, but if that is what the boss expected then it can be very hard to start explaining how the blogs are really being used to start conversations with influencers.

Ensure that the communications team and the people who will be named on the blogs understand how this works and what you are using as measures of success. If they have started thinking of themselves as publishing superstars because they see their name on a byline then you have a problem.

## Bureaucracy

I have had a client in the past that insisted on emailing the text that I could Tweet on their behalf. I would wait for emails to arrive featuring the approved text for tweets I could send out in their name.

This was an utterly ridiculous situation and would have been a lot simpler if the communications manager would just send the tweets - rather than emailing and asking me to send them on their behalf.

But the most common form of bureaucracy is over blog content. Every company will have an idea of the markets they are in and what business they are chasing at present. The marketing team might have a specific campaign they are working on themed on a geographic region or product. All this can overcomplicate the blogging process.

An example would be a typical current affairs comment. If The Economist magazine runs one of their in-depth analysis reports on your business area and a blog is drafted up giving a comment from the CEO on the Economist research, but then the communications director asks why the blog does not mention product X?

The writer will of course respond that it's not a product pitch, but a comment on something happening this week in the industry the company operates within. But if the communications team insists that all published commentary must mention campaign Y or product X, then suddenly your ability to present the CEO as a thought leader with an opinion is dragged away.

The writing team needs to agree with the communications team that there can be product or campaign specific blogs, but the blog should never read like an advert – it is not just an online press release.

These blogs are comments in the name of the CEO and should read as if he or she is thinking out loud about the industry – the best blogs ask a question or intentionally poke a stick into a subject and start a debate.

The communications team should also be able to approve content on behalf of the CEO. Most very senior executives are far too busy to approve every piece of content written in their name. They need to delegate some of this marketing authority to a trusted team.

If you can't get same-day approval most of the time on blogs then it will be difficult to ever say anything timely, especially when something important is happening in the industry that is clearly worth blogging about.

# Technophobia

I mentioned earlier in the book that no ghostwriter should ever pretend to be the CEO on a social media platform. While they can support the executive by drafting up ideas into blogs and pushing out some promotion on a tool such as Twitter, the real person must respond if anyone approaches the CEO on that Twitter account.

If your CEO has not bothered to install Twitter on their phone or iPad and has an expectation that all this social stuff is just looked after by the communications team, then your program is going to fail.

The CEO is almost certainly a busy person, but the point of supporting them with a writing team and people monitoring the key influencers is to build their own online influence. Whenever that requires that they really converse online with someone, it must be the real deal.

Besides, imagine the fun the press would have if they found out that any particular CEO was outsourcing their Twitter conversations to a ghostwriter because they just couldn't figure out how to use Twitter?

# Inadequate Commitment

I'm tempted to say that it is better to do nothing at all than to launch a project that is clearly inadequate. I have seen companies decide that 'something must be done' and therefore a blog is commissioned, but there is no budget for any engagement.

This usually creates a ghost blog. The blog exists and the CEO can be seen publishing – even if it is just once a month or even once a quarter – but there is no interaction. No readers will ever find the blog if no effort is made to help them find it.

The content itself creates a platform for engagement. If you are going to commission content and not budget for any engagement then it's rather like putting the cart before the horse. Either plan your content campaign in a way that allows for some engagement – it doesn't need an enormous budget to be effective - or rethink the entire project.

# Predicting disasters

All these potential points of failure can be anticipated in advance. They can be discussed with the communications team and the CEO in advance of the project commencing.

It is important to note that some of these problems will only occur once the project is underway and some – like scope creep – will occur because the project is suddenly seen as useful. The writing team can end up becoming victims of their own success.

Of all the potential issues I have listed, the most common is bureaucracy. If a company has never engaged on a serious blogging or social media program then they are likely to be very wary.

There are so many social horror stories in the media where communications managers want to lock down exactly who can and cannot speak on behalf of the company and the level of control can be so tough that any agile online conversation is impossible.

The issue faced by the UK division of global telecoms group Vodafone back in 2010 on their Twitter account is a good example of what can go wrong. On February 5th, 2010 Vodafone UK posted a shocking and homophobic message on their official @vodafoneuk Twitter account.

It was soon removed, but by the time it was taken offline, thousands of shocked Twitter users had passed the message on to their own online friends – asking if Vodafone had been hacked.

Vodafone communications went into crisis mode. The story made the international media and caused considerable brand damage to the firm. What could have happened?

It was a Friday. The marketing team at Vodafone were all away from their desks and someone in the office - who was enjoying their last day working at the company - noticed that the marketing team had left their computers logged into the main corporate Twitter account. So before leaving the office, the rogue staff member left a final note just to cause a stir.

He certainly caused a stir – globally. Vodafone was heavily criticized at the time for having such poor security over their corporate social media use that a member of staff with no connection to the Twitter team could pass by a desk in the office and just randomly leave offensive messages that were immediately published online in the company name.

Vodafone spent days apologizing to thousands of people. It was not a fatal mistake – they are a large company with a marketing budget to match, but a security slip like this could spell the end for a smaller organization.

Controlling who can send messages to Twitter on your behalf is a critical part of planning a social media strategy, but this needs to be balanced with an approvals procedure that allows proposed content to become approved content quickly enough for it to stay relevant to readers.

# Chapter 10: Making Your Content Strategy a Success

In chapter eight I explored the various ways that you can measure the success of a content-focused communication strategy. This will be different for every company and even every individual executive, but a general rule is that you always need to do more than just publishing.

If your 'strategy' is to publish a blog – and no more - then just hope that something comes from that alone, then good luck.

Think back to that old question, does a tree make any noise as it crashes to the ground in a forest if there is no person there to hear it? That's just like blogging.

There is so much content published online every single day now that if you don't do more than publishing alone then your own communications team may be the only readers. SEO is an important part of the answer for some content, but in this book I have focused mainly on B2B executives where it matters more about the quality of the readers rather than the quantity.

But what are the ingredients required to make your content strategy a success?

I suggest that there are five key factors you need to consider or address before embarking on this kind of strategy with your executive team.

1. **Know what you want to achieve.** You can't just start blogging because every executive has a blog. There needs to be a reason. What do you want to achieve? Is it important to increase the visibility of your executives as leaders or can you use their comments to interact with key influencers in your industry? This is of course related to how you measure success, but before you even start planning the indicators that you want to measure, you need some end goals – outcomes that can be achieved by creating blog content and using social media in this way.
2. **Get top level buy-in.** It's OK if this is the baby of the marketing team, but one day your boss is going to be at a major conference doing a Q&A and someone will ask about his or her Twitter posts from that morning. When they look dazed and confused because they have no idea what was on Twitter that morning, even though it was posted in their name, then you have a problem.
3. **Involve the management team.** Ensure that the managers who are being ghosted do at least have Twitter on their phones and do know what is being published on the blog. Ensure that they are interested in what's going on in their name. Above all, ensure that the program has authenticity.
4. **Communicate regularly.** The best ideas for content come from those at the front-line meeting the clients day after day – usually the sales team. They have views on the issues in the business and they can see a business story in Forbes or The Economist and tear it apart based on their own real-world experience. Make sure that you communicate regularly enough to capture these insights.
5. **Agree that it may take time to work.** It's going to take some time to build a following to the extent that

people are starting to consider your executives the go-to people for information on your industry – but it will happen. Ensure that they know it's not an overnight process and that there is support for the long-term.

You need to start your content endeavors with a basic knowledge of what it is that you want to achieve. As I have outlined earlier in this book, companies that have a relationship directly with their customers have a very different relationship with their customers to those B2B firms that just interact with other companies.

It's easier for a B2C company to engage in blogging and social activities that can be considered as just building the brand. For example, if Coca-Cola shares photos of cute babies wearing Coke branded clothes then it doesn't make you reach for the fridge, but it might make you share that image on your own social networks – therefore spreading the Coke message.

But executives in the B2B world probably need to do more than just brand building because they only have a limited number of customers anyway. If you run an HR consultancy, or a payroll service provider, or a contact center then your clients may be from a number of industries, but they will only ever be executives taking a decision on which company to hire for their business.

So an initial consideration about why you want to engage on a content strategy will naturally lead into how you are going to measure success.

It is essential that the executives involved in an online communication program using blogs or social media do know about what is being done and do support the initiative.

I have seen executives actively undermine the efforts of their marketing team by belittling the impact of social media on communications – even as the communications team is trying to position their boss as an online commentator.

Even if there is no intent to undermine these 'new' methods, ignoring the communication program can be just as damaging.

I once had a client with a very busy CEO (aren't they all?) This CEO was always too busy with clients and strategy to approve the blogs that were going to be published in his name. For about six months I churned out blog after blog commenting on the latest news in his industry sector and after all that time just one had been approved and posted on the blog, as I described earlier on in this book.

That client carried on paying my invoices. I was doing the work I had been contracted for, but they had a complete block internally. The CEO probably needed just two or three minutes to check and approve a 200-word blog, but he didn't rate it as a very important activity and therefore the entire program eventually collapsed when it became clear that he wasn't really bothered about a blog being published in his name.

Similarly I have published blogs for CEOs that are supportive of seeing articles published in their name, but they are not familiar with social networks.

Even as I write in 2014, I am still asked by some senior executives about hashtags # and the @ sign – 'what does it all mean' they ask me and it is clear that sometimes you have to go right back to basics. Like the early 1990s, when some executives would get their personal assistant to print out emails for them to answer by making notes on the printout.

If the executive you are working with is at this level of unfamiliarity with tools such as Twitter then training is an essential part of the program. They don't need to be tweeting and sharing photos all day, but when a journalist from the New York Times tweets a message to your boss, they should at least know how to respond without needing to ask.

The managers that are having content published in their name need to be aware of what is being published, when, and how they can help to support it. Many of these managers will have a LinkedIn profile even if they don't really use any other social networks – just because LinkedIn is seen as an essential place for every business person to house their identity today.

Instagram is a very useful tool for busy executives. Any busy executive with no time to write can still find a moment to take a photo using their phone. It could be the team in a remote office, or a conference crowd. Whatever the pictures, they can document life for that executive. The support team can monitor the photos and use them on the blog or tweet them.

It's also worth reminding executives who are thinking of photo-blogging in this way that Instagram has more users than Twitter and their Instagram account can be automatically linked to Twitter – so they can easily create new twitter posts just by taking photos.

But they can also use their LinkedIn profile to further promote their blogs, or to ensure that their other social networks – like Twitter – are promoted from their LinkedIn profile. Just a little support from the executive team can go a long way.

One of the issues that often crops up with executive blogging strategies is that of what to write about. When these programs are initially agreed, the manager or the communications team will send a list of topics over to the writing team and feel that this static list of eight or nine key topics will suffice. The problem is that it's often filled with very broad and generic topics such as strategy or business development.

The communications team needs to clarify the general scope with the writing team, so it is clear the type of topics that the manager wants to be seen writing about, but then the manager who has their name on the pieces should stay in touch. Even a very short email once a week saying how much they agree with the FT on one topic or disagree with CNN on another topic can help enormously.

These points of strong agreement or disagreement can even make great blogs in themselves as they create discussion. Imagine finding that your boss hates a big feature in Forbes and blogging about why they believe that one of the biggest business magazines in the world is wrong.

It's easy to tweet a link to your blog including Forbes and the author of their article. Maybe they will share it to their readers. Maybe they will comment. Either way, it's likely to create a conversation and that's great engagement with people who take an interest in your business.

All of this traction takes time to develop so it is important to agree on some breathing space or regular interim measures so you can show some growth along the way. Always stick to your guns regarding the measures of success though. Too many marketing executives believe that just increasing the number of followers on an account equals success.

I have had one client where I essentially had two bosses and two types of measurement – not ideal at all but typical in global companies full of dotted reporting lines.

The manager who had created the blogging program was very focused on the outcomes. He wanted to see that influencers noticed his blogs and commented on them or asked him out for a beer because of what he was saying online. But his colleagues in another part of the business were measuring the same blog and social media program based merely on numbers of followers.

I had to ride two horses, but I did point out that if all I wanted was followers then I could just pay a few dollars for an instant boost of thousands – that message eventually did sink in.

One client of mine was astounded to see his name listed in a trade magazine as one of the most influential bloggers in his industry – just months after commencing the blogging program.

This was a fantastic outcome and not something that I had coordinated at all. What happened was that his blogs and tweets had caused his Klout score to rapidly increase and the magazine was merely publishing a top 100 blogger list based on Klout as a measurement.

The only downside of this immediate success was that he then expected to be shortlisted for other awards without ever having written a blog in his life – and it didn't happen. Plus it meant I had to keep tracking his Klout score until I could convince him that it was really not all that important.

In another case, a client of mine decided to end our blogging agreement after just three months even though our contract was supposed to be for a year. During that brief time, the manager involved had gone from not using Twitter at all to having 500 followers – mostly in his industry.

Thanks to his blogs and tweets several trade magazine editors had contacted him and a couple of very senior industry analysts had been in touch asking about lunch.

For some, this would be an enormous success. Several key industry influencers were taking this boss more seriously within weeks of taking a more active approach to online discussion, however I guess he just assumed that a few tweets would lead to a new client within weeks.

# Chapter 11: Creating Your Own Content Strategy

You may have read all the way through this book so you are now brimming with ideas, or you might have just skipped to the end because your boss asked you to put a blogging strategy together by the end of the week.

Either way, it's worth summarizing the information into a step-by-step plan that you can build on depending on the specific requirements for your own organization.

## Define why exactly you want your CEO to blog

Before all else, stop and consider what it is that you really want to achieve. Corporate communications is changing fast and there are many trends and supposed experts advising on what you need to achieve.

Implementing a blogging strategy that involves regular public statements and engagement from your most senior executives affects how you view Public Relations and the media, Analyst Relations and communications with the people who write about your business in the most detail, bloggers and general business commentators or advisors - and your customers.

Blogging cuts across many communications channels that have been previously owned by various departments. Think about how the combined use of a blog and Twitter alone can allow the executive to easily reach employees, journalists, industry analysts, industry consultants and advisors, academics, bloggers, and existing or potential customers.

That's PR, AR, internal communications, corporate communications, marketing, and sales – all rolled into one.

So plan well and think about the scope of your ideas. You are going to be treading on some toes in well-established places.

## Define your expected outcomes

Are you trying to raise the profile of your CEO? Are you trying to raise the profile of the brand? Are you trying to reposition the brand? Are you trying to get more press coverage from journalists you don't normally interact with?

These are all valid questions. Once you have decided on the big picture argument about 'why' your executive team or CEO should be blogging, consider the quantifiable targets that you want to achieve.

It is easy to just write up a PowerPoint suggesting something like 'as a result of this blogging program, we expect to achieve improved press coverage', but these statements are vague and ill defined.

It's worth thinking also if you will need advice on how to improve your Search Engine Optimization (SEO). If you are creating new content you will probably want people to find it, so it's worth asking an SEO expert to improve the way your website and blog are designed. I have not explored SEO in depth in this book partly because it's not my own field of expertise, but also because it applies more to the larger audiences of B2C marketing. B2B blogging may involve smaller audiences, but they are influential people within the industry in question.

To explore the connection between SEO and Content Marketing in more detail I recommend Pam Didner's book "Global Content Marketing". In this book I have stayed within the scope of my own expertise, but Pam's book does explore how you can optimize websites based on the use of fresh content.

Think one year ahead. What should you have achieved that could not be achieved without the blogging program going ahead?

## Define how you will measure success

As I have repeated throughout this book, how you measure success depends very much on what you want to achieve, however I think it is extremely important to separate the achievement of the social network user and the achievement of the business executive.

By this I mean that 100 engaged and influential followers on Twitter can be far more important than 10,000 followers that are just bought or obtained by asking employees to follow the boss.

I have just mentioned the need to plan your expected outcomes. You need to plan for a future state, where will we be a year from now and what will the social media and blogging program have achieved?

Along the way to those outcomes there will be smaller events that you can measure as signs that your plan is succeeding, or at least moving in the right direction. These include influential contacts interacting with you, quoting you, or asking to meet in person.

Have you ended up being asked to contribute to a magazine or research report because of tweets? Has an influential analyst asked to meet because of your tweets?

Think about these small but real business outcomes and how they fit into the bigger picture. These outcomes will rarely be directly related to revenue, but will at least be positive improvements to your relationship with the people who directly influence your customers.

## Educate the team and get their buy-in

Make sure the executives are on board. They must support this because social media is very personal. Even if they have a ghostwriter supporting their blogs, when a business editor tweets a hello because they liked a blog it would be deceitful to have a PR, or the ghostwriter, answering tweets.

In addition, many executives still maintain a negative attitude about the use of social networks. Despite the maturity of these tools there is still a common misconception that only the young use them.

I was once asked to advise the partners of a major international consulting firm. The senior partners had been asked to tweet by their marketing and communications team. That was about as far as the guidance went – so the executives all installed Twitter on their mobile devices and started tweeting.

But after a few weeks, most of them gave up. They couldn't see the point. When I asked to see some of their tweets, it was obvious why. They were broadcasting details of their day – I just caught a train to Paris, I just arrived at the office, I am working on a complex presentation for a client... no wonder they were not attracting any followers or creating any engagement.

I told them to turn the entire process upside down, to start listening and to stop all that publishing of trivial information. In front of all the partners I took over the account of the most senior guy and asked him about some journals he reads, some journalists he respects, the analysts he turns to for detailed information on his area of expertise.

Within ten minutes I showed them how this executive now had a stream of information on his phone that was all published by people he respects or people that are useful for him to know professionally. He would be free to interact with any of those people, to create conversations based on what those people are saying.

The executive team at this firm was astonished, but all it took was a different look at how the discussions taking place online could be useful within the context of their business.

Executives are not using social networks because it's cool. They don't care about what teenagers are doing, but if the use of a network like Twitter can enable them to quickly and easily reach the key influencers in their business then it's not just a toy – it's an essential communication tool.

So, in addition to getting executive support, make sure that they really understand what you are doing and how they can support the program. Create some training guides, run some workshops, use videos if you can't get everyone together, but make it clear how the executives can use this to help improve their business.

Appendix A-D at the end of this book feature typical 'primers' I have used with executives when launching a blogging and social media program. These are short guides to what the overall plans are and how tools such as blogs, LinkedIn, and Twitter can help in particular.

## Define your scope and targets

Once the executive team is on board then you need to plan two key areas with them, what is the scope for the blog content and who are the people they want to see the blogs and other social interactions?

It is important to stress that the value of the blog itself is usually to position the individual executive as having their own mind and demonstrating competence in their business area – it should not read like a list of press releases for the business.

Think of it more like articles in a business magazine, commenting on the area of business you work in, rather than a series of posts that just says 'we do this well' or 'we are the cheapest in the market'.

A lot of this information regarding the scope may be with your marketing or PR teams anyway, but it's worth just asking the executives directly because they will have their name on the content that is published online. The key questions are:

- What subjects would you like the blog to cover or explore?
- How provocative would you like the blog to be – quite contrary to provoke more response, or just demonstrating competence in your subject area?
- Would you like to regularly comment on current affairs related to your business area in the blog?

When you have the scope for the blog content ready then you have a framework to operate within. You will know the preferred style of comment and the topics to comment on. The next area is the people who the executive would like to see the blog.

- Which individual journalists does the executive read?
- Which business or trade journals are most influential?
- Which industry analysts publish the most influential reports about your area of business?
- Which industry consultants recommend companies such as yours to their clients?
- Which bloggers and other experts write about your industry?

Create a "hit list" from the individuals and companies mentioned. This can be used on social networks, such as Twitter so relevant people can be monitored and informed about the blog – when appropriate.

# Define simple procedures everyone understands

Your exact procedures may differ depending on how you are interacting with the executive and what they want to achieve, but it is always best to keep it simple.

In social communications, things often move fast, so you cannot be checking an operations manual when making a decision on what to tweet or retweet.

Understanding how the writing and publishing procedures work is important for the day to day operation of the team, but is critically important when you need to hand off between the ghostwriter and the executive.

As an example, here is how I generally work with clients:

1. I agree the scope and targets as I outlined above.
2. I create the draft blog content and send to the client for approval.
3. Once approved, I'll upload the content.
4. I will then use the agreed social networks – usually Twitter and LinkedIn – to promote the blog content to the network of the executive.
5. I will generate other relevant content, such as tweets related to earlier blogs or recent news stories and also use the various social networks of the executive to reach out to people on the agreed influencer list.
6. If anyone responds and wants to have any form of conversation online – public or private – I inform the executive directly so they can hop onto their own social network and carry on the conversation.

These rules are fairly simple and easily understood. This framework allows me to work on behalf of an executive, creating blog content for them and giving them an active social media profile, but ensuring that when any interactions do take place online it really is that person – not a ghost – that is participating in the conversation.

## Define interim outcomes and review times

I talked earlier about a client who decided they had had enough of trying to make all this fancy social stuff work after a few weeks. Be realistic about what you can achieve.

Sometimes you will see enormous growth and interest in what you are doing and sometimes it will be fairly quiet, but use the strategic planning and expected outcomes to set some checkpoints where you can review what is working and what may need tweaking.

I recommend a review every quarter with a focus on:

- What actual business outcomes did we create in this quarter?
- Are we targeting the right influencers?
- Are people engaging with the content we create?

This allows a regular chance to improve the content, the way that you get that content in front of people, and whether the focus on business outcomes has slipped back into focusing on social media outcomes, i.e. the team has started focusing on followers rather than genuine outcomes.

# Chapter 12: Closing Thoughts

This is a book that is based entirely on my own experiences and I am primarily a writer, rather than a technologist. When someone asks for advice on search engine optimization (SEO) or how to redesign the look and feel of a blog, I call in the experts.

But I am a writer with a background in business. I've been there in the corporate world as a "road warrior" flying around the world managing people and spending more time eating airline food than relaxing in my own home.

I despair at much of the social media and blogging advice that I read from the self-proclaimed 'gurus' who have never had to manage anything more than their Facebook page. Being able to write great tweets doesn't necessarily win you any business and doesn't help you when times are hard and the HR director has asked you to lay off half of your team.

Making a real business work is much tougher than just tweeting great one-liners. I appreciate this and throughout this entire book I have tried to emphasize that the way people communicate is changing and so these social tools are an important topic, but they remain a tool for communication – not an end in itself.

In October 2014, one of my clients wrote me an email that included these words:

*"FYI we have won business that has been down to the blogs! And the LinkedIn blog [reuse] posts are driving opportunities as well."*

Nothing could be more satisfying than hearing this directly from a client and it goes straight to the heart of what I have tried to echo throughout this book. Social networking and media are fantastic communication tools that allow a new style of communication – anyone can publish their opinion today.

Anyone can use the Internet to check prices or reviews before making a purchase. Anyone can criticize a company online if they are unhappy with the service received.

Senior executives need to understand these tools because every executive in every company in every industry must have some relationship with their customers and this is now how customers are communicating.

But too often the social media advisers, experts, and gurus are focused on the process rather than outcomes. How many followers do you have? How many times were you retweeted? How many views has your blog achieved?

It's important to get an audience, but it is more important to get the right audience.

Andy Warhol famously said that everyone would be famous for fifteen minutes. But he never knew that eventually everyone would be a publisher in his or her own right.

What we are witnessing today is a change in the way we all communicate. Don't underestimate how this will affect your job. Tomorrow is never just yesterday plus another day.

Now go and start your next blog or build a strategy that will get your own executive team blogging.

# Appendix A

As mentioned earlier, appendices A-D feature typical 'primers' I have used with executives when launching a blogging and social media program. These are short guides to what the overall plans are and how tools such as blogs, LinkedIn, and Twitter can help in particular.

Feel free to copy and use these as guidelines for your own training notes. Each company will need something slightly different, as there will always be a different emphasis on how it should work, but these appendices offer a backbone of notes you can build on.

## A Social Media Overview

## Introduction

Social networking has grown into an important tool for business development. Tools such as LinkedIn are changing the way many companies find new employees and new business.

The aim of this short primer is to explain how you can benefit from the social media work [company or team name] already engages in and how you can help yourself to develop your own online network – without requiring much time.

Time is always the main reason for not engaging with social media, yet these networks are becoming too important to ignore. This guide aims to describe how you can be more involved, to the benefit of the company and yourself, without requiring a great time commitment.

# What are the benefits?

Social networks are where an enormous amount of business communication takes place today. Getting more involved can help the company – by demonstrating that we engage actively in these networks – and you personally as this engagement will be done using your own personal identity.

This helps to build your own personal brand, enhancing your own visibility in the industry

1. The key influencers in your industry are there, as well as the customers too.
2. Our customers often ask us for advice that involves modern technologies - such as social networks – they expect you to know what's going on.

For you, it's a push and pull. Your clients expect you to know about these technologies because they turn to you for advice.

But the advantage of more online activity is often overlooked by those in business development because social networks are often seen as platforms for publishing, you need to publish all the time, telling people your latest meal, how you are stuck in traffic etc.

Turn that on its head and remember that you can use this tool to monitor every important journalist, analyst, and advisor in your business – they are all on there. Then interact with them. No need to talk about breakfast - or anything else – just engage with people.

# What works now?

The social network environment is fast moving, but there is some stability over the networks favored for business. This could – and will – change in a few years, but lets focus on what works now. These are:

- **Twitter:** used for discussions, communication.
- **LinkedIn:** used for business networking and sharing business news.
- **Blogging:** blogs in general are useful as a way of demonstrating your own credibility in the industry. These are not sales pitches, just you making a regular comment on the news or trends in the business. A blog is useful because when you attempt to kick off discussions in the other networks the blog gives you something as a base – it is a catalyst.

In addition, there is a blogging platform within LinkedIn that many people have not noticed. Go to the 'home' page then look at the status bar:

That pencil icon means 'publish a blog'. If you write a blog within LinkedIn, it is easy for your network to see and can be shared to all the groups that you participate in – a very powerful way to share your ideas.

# Conclusion

Even if you get most of your business from personal relationships, an enhanced profile on social media allows you to stay in touch more often with your important connections and to reach out more effectively to industry influencers. What should you do first?

1. **Register a Twitter account in your name.** Search for and follow some key influencers in your business area such as the analysts, journalists, trade journal editors, bloggers. Put the Twitter app on your phone. It will be news entirely from the thoughts of the influencers in your business area.
2. **Get a LinkedIn profile if you don't have one.** Make sure you go and follow our company page on LinkedIn. Check out the blog functionality and consider what you might want to say.
3. **Think of two or three blog ideas and suggest them to marketing team.** Trends, a reaction to news, or other comment are ideal – we are demonstrating ideas and thought leadership – creating conversations about the business.

This primer is exactly that – an introduction. We believe that the industry is changing and we can use social media to not only get more business through better communication with influencers, but we also need to do this because our business environment demands that our team understands these technologies.

# Appendix B

## Blogging

## Introduction

Blogging has come a long way since it's birth about 15 years ago as little more than a way to publish online diaries. Now blogs, magazines, and online newspapers are almost synonymous, all blurring together to create opinion online. News aggregators – like Google News – now treat many blogs as important news sources in their own right.

Publishing your own blogs that offer your thoughts and industry opinion can be a powerful tool when trying to open the door of a new prospect – and can help to ensure that key influencers also notice what you are doing.

## Value for Our Company

We publish blogs on our main corporate site here [blog site].

Most of the engagement for our team comes from the LinkedIn and Twitter social networks, however the blog gives a platform to speak about the industry. By having views, and an opinion, it is far easier to approach industry influencers on the social networks as they can see we are also blogging our own thoughts.

We publish [x] new blogs every week and any member of the team is welcome to suggest ideas.

## What do we blog about?

It's easier to say what we don't blog about. It's not a direct hard pitch for our services. What we want to use the blog for is to establish your own credentials as thought leaders and experts in the industry.

It is often possible for us to take the blog content and to place it in other industry journals or blogs – giving the content an additional life and new audience that would not be possible if all we did was say 'buy from us.'

## Getting your blog online

Send your comments and ideas to [team member]. In particular ideas related to business areas you are focused on, commenting on current affairs or commenting on industry data produced by analysts allows us to craft a blog that provokes further discussion.

You do not need to write 300 words – just the idea or a link to a news story and a short note saying 'this is wrong because' or 'I agree because' is enough for us to create the text – you can then check the draft before it ever goes live.

## Alternative routes

LinkedIn has a built-in blogging platform called Pulse. You can quickly take a blog that is crafted for the main corporate blog page and then re-publish it on your own LinkedIn – ensuring that your entire business network will also see it.

In addition, you can reach out to bloggers or editors of trade journals in your own area to ask if they would be interested in using some of the content you are publishing on the corporate blog – this is possible so long as we keep your comment focused on the industry rather than just being a comment on our services. It's not an advert.

# Appendix C

## LinkedIn

## Introduction

LinkedIn has grown over a decade or so to become the biggest global professional networking site on the Internet. Having a well-crafted profile on LinkedIn has largely replaced the need for a résumé as many employers now actively seek new employees on the site.

LinkedIn also allows professionals to build up and maintain connections to all their professional contacts. The 'Connections' app in particular is a great download for your phone. It monitors your entire business network and lets you know who is changing job, who has a work anniversary, and who you should send a birthday greeting.

## Blogging on LinkedIn

LinkedIn recently added a blogging capability inside the system – part of the LinkedIn Pulse news network. Pulse started out as a business magazine within LinkedIn where very influential leaders could blog. Now anyone can add his or her own blog, vastly increasing the amount of business news within the system.

Your blog can be immediately shared with your own professional network and any business groups you participate in and if it looks like it will be of wide general interest it is likely that the LinkedIn editors will share it using their news pages.

It is a very powerful way to re-use the blogs you create for the corporate blog – in addition to any other blogs you may want to create – because all that time cultivating a network on LinkedIn means you now have the perfect audience to share your views with.

## How does it work?

Go to the 'home' page inside LinkedIn then look at the status bar:

That pencil icon means 'publish a blog'. Click the pencil, type in the content and then click publish – that's it. It is a useful idea to also add a striking photo into your blog because the photo will be displayed with the headline.

As many photos are subject to copyright and cannot be just stolen and used it's advisable to use a photo network such as Flickr. Use the search function to find a suitable photo with the 'Creative Commons' option on – Getty Images also offer CC Royalty-free legal photos.

Creative Commons is like a copyright system for people who freely share their photographs, so you can legally use the images.

https://www.flickr.com/
http://www.gettyimages.com/creativeimages/royaltyfree

# Appendix D

## Twitter

## Introduction

Twitter is a fantastic tool for conversation – it's an engagement network. Don't fall into the common trap of believing that it requires you to spend endless hours publishing the minutiae of your daily life.

You can be active on Twitter without publishing details of your breakfast or commute to the office.

## News Curation

One of the most important features of Twitter is the concept of a 'curated list' of information. If you create a new Twitter account now, then your timeline will be blank – you need to start following some people so their updates tick through the timeline creating information you can interact with.

Think of the people you value. The journals, the journalists, and the industry analysts – they are all on Twitter. You can create a timeline of information that is coming direct from all these people meaning you have created a curated list of news that should be useful - and interesting.

# Engagement

You can just watch the news, reading the updates from that list of interesting users, but the real value comes from interaction – you can engage with other users.

Imagine your timeline contains information from influencers such as:

- Business and industry-specific journalists
- Industry analysts focused on your specialist area
- Bloggers and other experts with a large audience
- Consultants who advise clients on which company to work with – when our company may be on that list
- Peers in similar companies

Imagine you see a New York Times writer tweeting negatively about your industry. You can immediately tweet the journalist back and suggest that maybe they should meet your team?

Or you see an international industry analyst tweet that he or she is arriving in your city for a conference and has an afternoon to spare. You can tweet the analyst and suggest a coffee or beer.

The possibilities are clearly endless, but the idea is that with Twitter allowing you to easily monitor these influencers, it is easy to reach out with ideas to them.

# Finding People

Sometimes it's easy. Use Google to type a contact name plus Twitter and it will usually tell you their Twitter ID.

But if you want to search all of Twitter for people interested in specific keywords and topics then **manageflitter.com** is a tool worth checking.

# Appendix E

As a final afterthought, I have included a Huffington Post article I wrote in February 2014. This article led to me thinking further and writing the book based on these ideas.

**Huffington Post – 21 Feb 2014**
**http://j.mp/ghostblogger**

### *Is It Possible to 'Ghostblog' for a Leading CEO?*

I'm about to write a new book about blogging. Really, it's about the art of ghost-blogging and the experience I have of this hidden corporate culture that allows C-level executives to be prolific commentators on their industry.

I mentioned this on my Facebook recently and a friend said I should describe the birth of the book. What's the first step? How will I plan what I want to say? So here are a few thoughts that may answer some of those questions.

I have been blogging now for over a decade. In fact, I have watched blogs mutate from the original form of 'web-logging' that was just like keeping an online diary to the present-day where most people get their news about the world from blogs.

My blogging has taken many forms. I started out just making diary notes on LiveJournal like everyone else. Then I found that a blog was actually a great way to save news stories that I wanted to refer back to later - lots of sites developed later to do that more efficiently.

I used to keep a regular blog on myspace, but since they relaunched I guess I've lost all those posts and I have hundreds of entries now on my personal blog, which is really just random thoughts and observations.

What changed it for me was when I started blogging first for the technology magazine Computing, and later on, Computer Weekly. I got these blogging gigs because I was known as a technology author - I had written several books about IT, outsourcing, and the globalization of the technology business so the magazines gave me a platform.

Computing never paid me, and Computer Weekly paid based only on page views - which meant that to earn anything meaningful would require enormous traffic to my blog. But I'm not complaining about that; here I am blogging now for the Huffington Post and like all the other HuffPo bloggers, I don't get paid for it.

Along the way I also became a regular political blogger for Reuters and I was twice shortlisted as UK business blogger of the year by Computer Weekly. I never actually won, but it's the shortlists that count isn't it?

All this visibility as a known writer of books and blogs led to me getting calls from companies who wanted to be seen on the Internet. They could engage the services of a PR firm, but then it would be difficult to capture the real voice of their executives when a professional PR is blogging on their behalf.

It was suggested to me that as I was a writer who had also been a senior manager in the technology industry in the past and had experience of outsourcing and IT operations all over the world, maybe I could ghostwrite a blog for a technology CEO?

This happened more than once and I soon found that I was blogging away in the voice of various CEOs. When Twitter came along I even started tweeting on behalf of some of them, but never engaging people in tweeted conversation - that was a golden rule.

One day in 2008, the BBC's technology editor Rory Cellan-Jones asked me to appear on Radio 4's Today program to talk about all of this. I argued then that it was really no different to a politician getting their speech ghostwritten and I still believe that, but it is a conditional belief.

Social networks are very personal. A CEO can be supported by a ghostwriter feeding blogs and extra content to him or her, but if the executive has no interest in using this kind of communication tool then it's not possible to fake their presence just by tweeting links to news articles and hoping that this can pass for 'engagement.'

So, I'm about to write about what works and doesn't work when executives blog. Today the wider world of corporate blogging is often called content marketing, but I'm going to focus mostly on executives who want to be seen blogging.

I sat down last week and drafted ten chapter headings, then wrote a summary of each one. Now I'm listing ideas I want to cover in each chapter. Over the next few weeks, I'll tackle each chapter one by one and hopefully have a first draft early in March.

This is not going to be a detailed academic study. I'm not going to interview or even name the CEOs I have worked with, but it will all be based on the real experience of a ghostwriter who has written online for dozens of senior executives in companies all over the world.

# References:

Didner, Pam. Global Content Marketing: How to Create Great Content, Reach More Customers, and Build a Worldwide Marketing Strategy that Works, McGraw Hill 2015

Holiday, Ryan. Trust me I'm lying: Confessions of a Media Manipulator, Portfolio 2012

Lovell, Nicholas. The Curve: From Freeloaders into Superfans: The Future of Business, Portfolio Penguin 2013

Postman, Neil. Amusing Ourselves to Death: Public Discourse in the Age of Show Business, Penguin 1985

### Preface
1
http://thenextweb.com/socialmedia/2014/10/19/content-marketing-trends-business-implementing/

2
http://www.nytimes.com/2014/10/27/business/media/how-facebook-is-changing-the-way-its-users-consume-journalism.html

3 http://www.nydailynews.com/new-york/twitter-user-star-airways-crash-janis-krums-sets-internet-abuzz-iphone-photo-article-1.408174

4 https://twitter.com/ruskin147

### Chapter 2
1 https://www.youtube.com/watch?v=QlKz4b7IeG4

2 http://www.washingtonpost.com/blogs/monkey-cage/wp/2014/04/07/the-less-americans-know-about-ukraines-location-the-more-they-want-u-s-to-intervene/

3 http://www.huffingtonpost.com/mark-hillary/

4  https://www.youtube.com/user/russellbrand
5
    http://www.theguardian.com/media/2014/feb/20/mail-online-traffic-metro-standard-mirror
6
    http://www.nytimes.com/2014/12/16/nyregion/riches-to-rags-for-new-york-teenager-as-a-story-falls-apart.html

7  http://www.riverpoolsandspas.com/

8  http://contentmarketinginstitute.com/what-is-content-marketing/

**Chapter 4**
1  http://events.usefulsocialmedia.com/docs/top-10-predictions.pdf
2  http://techcrunch.com/2006/09/26/facebook-just-launched-open-registrations/

**Chapter 7**
1  https://twitter.com/richardbranson
2
    https://twitter.com/sirrogermoore/status/525161838934511616

www.markhillary.com